for Maureen,
"who on the river about you throw
a calm *solificatio*,
a warmth throughout the universe..."
(see p. 81) –

much love,
Lucy
May 1990

Auden's Apologies for Poetry

Auden's Apologies for Poetry

Lucy McDiarmid

PRINCETON UNIVERSITY PRESS
PRINCETON, NEW JERSEY

Published by Princeton University Press, 41 William Street,
Princeton, New Jersey 08540
In the United Kingdom: Princeton University Press, Oxford

Library of Congress Cataloging-in-Publication Data

McDiarmid, Lucy.
Auden's apologies for poetry / Lucy McDiarmid.
p. cm.
1. Auden, W. H. (Wystan Hugh), 1907–1973—Criticism and interpretation. 2. Auden, W. H. (Wystan Hugh), 1907–1973—Aesthetics. 3. Poetry. I. Title.
PR6001.U4Z757 1990 811'.52—dc20 89-10660

ISBN 0-691-06784-8 (alk. paper)

Publication of this book has been aided by a grant from the Paul Mellon Fund of Princeton University Press

This book has been composed in Linotron Sabon

Princeton University Press books are printed on acid-free paper, and meet the guidelines for permanence and durability of the Committee on Production Guidelines for Book Longevity of the Council on Library Resources

Printed in the United States of America by Princeton University Press, Princeton, New Jersey
10 9 8 7 6 5 4 3 2 1

FOR PHILIP J. ESCOLL

. . . love, or truth in any serious sense,
Like orthodoxy, is a reticence.

Contents

Preface ix

Acknowledgments xv

Abbreviations xix

INTRODUCTION
The Finest Tumbler of His Day 3

CHAPTER ONE
Pardon and "Pardon" 14

CHAPTER TWO
The Generous Hour: Poems and Plays of the 1930s 46

CHAPTER THREE
The Other Side of the Mirror: *New Year Letter, For the Time Being*, and *The Sea and the Mirror* 73

CHAPTER FOUR
Apologies for Poetry: Poems 1948–1973 119

CONCLUSION
Writing This for You to Open When I Am Gone 159

Appendix: The Manuscript Drafts of New Year Letter, *Part III, Opening Passage* 169

Index 173

Preface

> If good literary critics are rarer than good poets or novelists, one reason is the nature of human egoism. A poet or novelist has to learn to be humble in the face of his subject matter which is life in general. But the subject matter of a critic, before which he has to learn to be humble, is made up of authors, that is to say, of human individuals, and this kind of humility is much more difficult to acquire. It is far easier to say—"Life is more important than anything I can say about it"—than to say—"Mr. A's work is more important than anything I can say about it."
>
> —Auden, "Reading"

AUDEN'S WORK is more important than anything I can say about it.

In so encouraging the modesty of literary critics, Mr. A. did not altogether debar their efforts. In spite of "human egoism," Auden conceded, a critic can perform a number of valuable services, such as giving a " 'reading' of a work which increases my understanding of it" (*DH* 8). This book offers a reading of Auden's work, based in part on Auden's own self-commentary: on essays that talk about art, on poems that talk about themselves, on poems that rewrite and revise earlier poems by Auden.

"Goody." So Auden commented to Christopher Isherwood as the boat-train pulled out of London on 18 January 1939, as he left behind the idealisms of the thirties, all political and social concerns, and the "magnificent early lyrics," to become an unserious poet, or, worse still, a minor poet, his poems empty, agreeable contrivances. Or so the story goes. Spoiled by the intensities of apocalypse, Auden's critics distort and misread some of his greatest work. It is like complaining that *Top Hat* is not *The Seventh Seal*, or *As You Like It Götterdämmerung*: comic genius may be mistaken for triviality, and dazzling complexities of self-reference for mere ingenuity, by those who prefer their tone-colors dark.

Auden was never more intensely interested in thinking about ultimate value, and in defining literature's relation to such value, than in the ten or fifteen years after he immigrated to New York (he called himself "a New Yorker," not an American). Freed from the obligation to criticize and reform the society of his native country, Auden devoted his imaginative energies to commentary on art. And about art he was never complaisant: with greater consistency than he had ever used to undermine "bourgeois" society, Auden undermined literature. Every major poem and every major essay become a *retractio*, a statement of art's frivolity, vanity, and guilt.

Not that Auden did not occasionally attribute positive values to art—it could "delight, sadden, disturb, amuse, instruct"—but such powers were never ultimate (*DH* 60). Somewhere, Auden's poems suggest, lies a realm of value that poetry can invoke only by implication, debunking its own pretensions to meaning.

> All the rest is silence
> On the other side of the wall;
> And the silence ripeness,
> And the ripeness all.
>
> (*CP* 352)

So *The Sea and the Mirror* at its opening attributes to silence, not to words, the "ripeness" that is meaning. The far side of the wall is outside the poem, off the page, a location that cannot be indicated except to say that it is not here, not in this poem.

Later Auden, New Yorker Auden, was a practicing Episcopalian, but he was not an apologist for the Anglican Communion. His impulse was not to magnify God's powers but to delimit art's. Calling poetry a game, denying it moral authority, insisting that "No artist, qua artist, can understand what is meant by *God is love* or *Thou shalt love thy neighbor* because he doesn't care whether god and men are loving or unloving," Auden in his prose statements differentiates poetry from other systems of meaning (*DH* 456). With a certain aphoristic punch, Auden denies poetry therapeutic, supernatural, and heroic powers: "Catharsis is properly effected, not by works of art, but by religious rites" (*DH* 27); "Poetry is not magic" (*DH* 27); "We live in a new age in which the artist neither can have . . . unique heroic importance nor believes in the Art-God enough to desire it" (*EF* 150).

Auden writes against the grain of most people who talk about art. To defend the creation of poetry only as the "right to play, the right to frivolity" requires courage in a culture that takes its art seriously (*DH* 89). People like to think that art is improving and criticism inspirational. A recent work of literary criticism is called a "remarkable gift . . . for all who read poetry to stay alive, to be consoled, to be made braver."[1] A contemporary poet writes that "poetry can be as potentially redemptive and possibly as illusory as love."[2] And a contemporary playwright sounds like Auden in the thirties, pausing wishfully at the threshold where "affect" becomes political action: "I think theater can make people *feel*. Then they'll decide what to do."[3]

Auden's justification of frivolity is not frivolous: it always provides the occasion for a ranking of values. The peasant, notes Auden,

> may play cards in the evening while the poet writes verses, but there is one political principle to which they both subscribe, namely, that among the half dozen or so things for which a man of

[1] Gloria Emerson, review of *Praises and Dispraises* by Terrence Des Pres, as quoted in *Penguin Paperbacks: Literature Catalog 1989* (New York, 1988), 68.

[2] Seamus Heaney, *The Government of the Tongue: The 1986 T. S. Eliot Memorial Lectures and Other Critical Writings* (New York, 1989), xxii.

[3] Terrence McNally, as quoted in Patricia Leigh Brown, "Twenty Playwrights Survey Urban Life," *New York Times*, 19 June 1988, Arts and Leisure section.

> honor should be prepared, if necessary, to die, the right to play, the right to frivolity, is not the least. (*DH* 89)

The social gap between poet and peasant must be acknowledged before their common right to harmless private pleasures can be insisted on. Yet differences of class are not adduced as an evil that art reflects or ignores or ought to remedy; the very instancing of a "peasant" rather than a "worker" shows that Auden is not thinking ideologically. Social differences are subordinated to a shared "political principle." Even the articulation of that principle implies degrees of significance: the "right to play" may be one of six things worth dying for, but Auden will not say it's the worthiest. Art just is not that important. But it is not "not the least." And this putative "man of honor" ought not to be imagined as eager for some romantic sacrifice; he is only prepared "if necessary" to die for the right to play. More nuanced than Liberty, Equality, and Fraternity, this principle circumscribes frivolity as much as it politicizes it.

Auden's apologies for poetry advertise their exclusions. Poetry is justified insofar as it undermines its own importance and invokes less frivolous realms. "It's rather a privilege," he writes in the elegy for Louis MacNeice, "to serve this unpopular art," because

> . . . our handful
> of clients at least can rune. (It's heartless to forget about
> the underdeveloped countries,
> but a starving ear is as deaf as a suburban optimist's . . .)
> (*AH* 10)

The parentheses supply a weight of meaning here: Auden is not heartless and he has not forgotten the starving. In fact, he cannot justify his art without reminding himself that he writes for a well-fed elite. The parentheses indicate what happens when the poet is exercising the right to frivolity: moral issues are relegated to parenthetical status. The politics in the foreground of the 1930s remain in the background of the 1950s and 1960s, in double negatives and in parentheses. Because he respects the sufferings of the hungry, Auden refuses to argue that poetry is remedial.

And beyond the audience that poetry can never address, and the ills it can never cure, lies an ultimate religious truth it can never express. Having invoked the starving whom it is "heartless to forget," "The Cave of Making" names another inability: "Speech can at best, a shadow echoing / the silent light, bear witness / to the Truth it is not" (*AH* 10).

An appropriate criticism of Auden would also rank values, keeping in mind not only Auden's belief in the secondary status of art ("Life is more important than anything I can say about it") but his belief in the tertiary status of criticism ("Mr. A's work is more important than anything I can say about it"). Like poetry, literary criticism is a privilege, justifiable as the "right to play, the right to frivolity." By reading Auden, who confidently calls poetry frivolous and playful, this book can indulge in the elaborate and harmless pleasures of criticism, acknowledging here its separation from the larger extrapoetic world where, as Auden says, heroes roar and die, and the "lion's mouth whose hunger / No metaphors can fill" waits to be satisfied.

Acknowledgments

OVER THE LAST TEN YEARS David Bromwich's friendship has been important to me, and his 1986 article "Recent Work in Literary Criticism" continues to be a source of pleasure and sustenance; I reread it to be repersuaded that literary critics can occasionally be useful. While I was working on this book, Daniel Hoffman, Samuel Hynes, and Yopie Prins listened, read, suggested, and advised generously and intelligently. I am grateful for their knowledge of Auden and for their help. Stanley Hopper and Timothy Materer also read the manuscript with great care and offered many good ideas for its improvement. A long time back, Philip Winsor suggested I write a book like this, and I thank him for that initial push.

In daily kindnesses, friendly interest, and practical help, the late Joseph P. McGowan of Villanova University was an incomparable colleague. His intellectual energy was an inspiration, and his irony a comfort. Sterling F. Delano, the Reverend Kail C. Ellis, O.S.A., and the Reverend Lawrence C. Gallen, O.S.A., all of Villanova University, helped my work on this book considerably by allowing me reduced teaching loads and flexible schedules.

Many other people have helped with a number of matters, ranging from the nitty-gritty to the grand. Some of them discussed Auden with me; others ransacked their shelves to find references; and all were happily amenable to telephone conversations at all hours of the day and night. I'd like to name and thank them: William C. Edinger and Edward Mendelson especially, and also Fern Brown, Kim Brown, Michael Durkan, Anne Gallagher, John Hunt, Beatrice Mitchell, Nan Mulford, Georgia Nugent, Phillip Pulsiano, Evan Radcliffe, Nancy Shaw, Cathy Staples, David Tatarsky, and Marie Teehan. Spencer and Ardie Callender made the maple sugar candy that enabled me to concentrate on this book for long hours at a time. And although there's nothing Irish about Auden, I'd like to mention, at least collectively, my friends in the American Conference for Irish Studies, because they talk about poets and poetry with such energy and love.

For making available Auden's manuscripts in the Berg Collection of the New York Public Library I am grateful to its curator, Lola Szladits, and to Patrick Lawlor and Brian McInerney. John P. Chalmers of the Harry Ransom Humanities Research Center, The University of Texas at Austin, deserves special mention for his courage in reading me long passages in Auden's handwriting over the telephone. Cathie Brettschneider of Princeton University Press has been calm, wise, and patient. Jane Taylor copyedited with exemplary tact.

I want to include thanks to my daughters, Emily and Katharine, for being themselves, lovable and good-natured, and to my husband, Harris B. Savin, whose piquant and irreverent comments on a subject in which he had little interest were so astute that they turned out to be helpful.

Portions of chapters 1 and 3 first appeared in "Artifice and Self-Consciousness in Auden's *The Sea and the Mirror*," *Contemporary Literature*, © The University of Wisconsin Press (1975). A shorter version of chapter 2 first appeared in *Modern Language Quarterly* 46 (1985) as "Auden's 1931 Epithalamion and Other Generous Hours." I would like to thank the editors of both journals for permission to reprint revised versions of these articles.

Grateful acknowledgment is made to the following for permission to quote from copyrighted material: for unpublished passages from Auden's letters and manuscripts, the Henry W. and Albert A. Berg Collection, The New York Public Library, Astor, Lenox, and Tilden Foundations, Swarthmore College Library, and the Harry Ransom Humanities Research Center, The University of Texas at Austin; unpublished writings by Auden are copyright © 1990 by The Estate of W. H. Auden and may not be reprinted without written permission. Nonexclusive rights in the English language throughout the British Commonwealth have been granted by Faber and Faber Publishers for excerpts from *Collected Poems* and *The English Auden: Poems, Essays and Dramatic Writings 1927–1939*. For permission to quote from the copyrighted works of W. H. Auden, permission has been granted for U.S. and Canadian rights by Random House, Inc.

Abbreviations

AH	*About the House*
CLP	*Collected Longer Poems*
CP	*Collected Poetry* (1945)
CWW	*City without Walls*
DBS	*The Dog beneath the Skin*
DD	*The Dance of Death*
DH	*The Dyer's Hand*
EA	*The English Auden*
EF	*The Enchafèd Flood*
EG	*Epistle to a Godson*
FA	*Forewords and Afterwords*
HC	*Homage to Clio*
N	*Nones*
SA	*Shield of Achilles*
SW	*Secondary Worlds*
TYF	*Thank You, Fog*

Auden's Apologies for Poetry

INTRODUCTION

The Finest Tumbler of His Day

Listen, good people, and you shall hear
A story of old that will gladden your ear,
The Tale of Barnaby, who was, they say,
The finest tumbler of his day.
—Auden, "The Ballad of Barnaby"

BY SOME ACCOUNTS Auden was the finest tumbler of his day.

"The Ballad of Barnaby," a libretto written for the students of a Connecticut prep school in 1969, constitutes a nostalgic apology for poetry (*EG* 42–46). Barnaby's spiritual history is Auden's as it would have been in a simpler world, the kind of world in which poems like "The Ballad of Barnaby" are not written.

This *faux-naïf* narrative—illustrated by Edward Gorey in 1972—tells the story of a religious awakening.[1] Barnaby is a performer, pleasing the crowd with his gymnastic feats: "The French Vault, the Vault of Champagne, / The Vault of Metz, and the Vault of Lorraine." Sexual, charming, attractive, Barnaby tumbles in order to charm and to attract:

His eyes were blue, his figure was trim,
He liked the girls and the girls liked him;
For years he lived a life of vice,
Drinking in taverns and throwing the dice.
(*EG* 42)

Such is Barnaby's life, frivolous and immoral, until one day when he is "riding / Between two cities"—two cities of a very

[1] A copy of "The Ballad of Barnaby," illustrated by Edward Gorey, was handed out at the memorial service for Auden in the Cathedral of St. John the Divine in New York. Daniel Hoffman kindly gave me his copy.

probably Augustinian nature. Passing two ravens over a body hung on a gallows, Barnaby experiences a kind of enlightenment; that is, he gets frightened. The ravens taunt him with the prospect of Hell, and he repents: "Woe is me! I will forsake / This wicked world and penance make." Barnaby enters a monastery and joins the brothers in their communal life.

Or, as the poem says, "they let him in"—Barnaby is not immediately assimilated into this society. The monks are all literary sophisticates: they write and decorate manuscripts and sing prayers in several languages. "Now Barnaby had never learned to read": feeling inarticulate and inferior, the illiterate Barnaby seeks out a statue of the Virgin in the crypt and addresses her:

> "Blessed Virgin," he cried, "enthroned on high,
> Ignorant as a beast am I:
> Tumbling is all I have learnt to do;
> Mother-of-God, let me tumble for You."
>
> (*EG* 44)

Before the statue Barnaby performs the same acts he used to charm the crowds with: "The French Vault, the Vault of Champagne, / The Vault of Metz and the Vault of Lorraine." As he sinks exhausted to the ground, the Virgin steps out of her niche: " 'Thank you, Barnaby,' She said and smiled; / 'Well have you tumbled for me, my child.' "

Daily thereafter, during prayers at the canonical hours, Barnaby goes to the crypt and tumbles before the Virgin. Curious to find where Barnaby disappears to, the Abbot follows him, watches, and decides, "This man is holy and humble." One day Barnaby cries out to the Virgin, "I beg of Thee / To intercede with Thy Son for me!" He performs a final vault and drops dead. Rushing to carry him off to Hell, "grinning demons" insist, "every tumbler belongs to us." But Our Lady intercedes, of course, and angels bear Barnaby's soul to heaven.

This is Auden's portrait-of-the-artist-as-tumbler. Like Caliban (in *The Sea and the Mirror*) with his "incorrigible staginess," like the young boy in "In Praise of Limestone," pleasing and teasing, "displaying his dildo," confident of his charms, Barnaby performs—initially—out of vanity, seeking love and admiration from his audience. His "life of vice" consists of simple sensual pleasures and immediate gratifications. The ravens awaken Barnaby's conscience and force him to put his pleasures and vanities in a spiritual context. So—as the straightforward narrative of Auden's ballad says—Barnaby knocks at the door of a monastery "and they let him in."

Tumbling before the Virgin, Barnaby does not change his talent; as Auden says in the title poem of *Epistle to a Godson*, the volume in which "The Ballad of Barnaby" appears, "All pleasures come from God." What changes is the philosophical ground of Barnaby's performance. His vaulting, originally part of a guilty "staginess," a narcissistic showing-off of his blue eyes and trim figure, a mode of seduction, becomes an act of worship and homage. Like Auden who wrote a series of poems situated at each of the *Horae Canonicae*, Barnaby tumbles for the Virgin "at the Office-Hours." Although the "statue of Our Lady" is "carved in wood," Barnaby speaks as if addressing a living presence, invoking her as "Blessed Virgin" and "Mother-of-God." She is his Elizabeth Mayer, his limestone, his Clio, the holy maternal being who sanctifies his gift. (Elizabeth Mayer, who plays Beatrice to Auden's Dante in *New Year Letter*, was a German refugee and good friend to whom Auden gave a baby picture of himself in his mother's arms.)[2] Barnaby still performs for approval, for acceptance, for love, but with a sense of unworthiness and of need for a sanction beyond himself. No longer a gambling, alcoholic seducer, "This man is holy and humble." Performed reverentially, the tumbling defers to and derives its meaning from a spiritual being outside human arts and skills.

Tumbling—or so it would appear—signifies all artistic talents because it is beautiful, because it is a gift, and because it so demonstrably has no spirituality in itself. But the paradigm

[2] Auden inscribed the picture, "Elizabeth. I know my mother would be (and is) very happy to see who has taken her place." See Humphrey Carpenter, *W. H. Auden: A Biography* (Boston, 1981), 314.

offered by the poem is nostalgic and regressive: it is a paradigm of the conversion Auden could never have. Barnaby can be holy and humble because he is illiterate, "Ignorant as a beast," and therefore also innocent as a beast. The monks will never experience the personal blessing of the Virgin; their very literacy denies them access:

> The Abbot could logically define
> The place of all creatures in the Scheme Divine.
>
> Brother Maurice then wrote down all that he said
> In a flowing script that it might be read,
> And Brother Alexander adorned the book
> With pictures that gave it a beautiful look.
>
> (*EG* 43)

Their learning puts the monks at several removes from the Deity: Brother Maurice transcribes the words of the Abbot, not the words of God. All these schemes and definitions and decorations constitute deficiencies in a poem that celebrates the spontaneous, the physical, the ignorant. Learned and logical, the monks, like the literate Auden, can observe and describe the Barnabys of the world, but the textuality of their talents will forever create barriers between themselves and divinity.

Barnaby's is, of course, a broadly idealized conversion. Barnaby never articulates his emergent awareness; he simply gets scared and redirects his energies to the Virgin. The poem makes it clear that Barnaby's ignorance and newfound humility inspire the Virgin to step forward. The Abbot dubs him "holy," so—to revise Caliban—Barnaby's staginess is corrigible. But Auden and his more sophisticated personae, like Caliban, or the Wise Men of *For the Time Being*, or the poet who mourns Louis MacNeice in "The Cave of Making," exist in a more complex philosophical system. Their vanity is inextricable from their art. Showing off on the stage of the text, with flowing scripts and marginal decorations, they can only achieve greater awareness of their incorrigibility.

In the "Postscript" to the elegy for MacNeice, Auden talks about his own art as if he were the younger, naughtier Barnaby:

Time has taught you
how much inspiration
your vices brought you,
what imagination
can owe temptation
yielded to,
that many a fine
expressive line
would not have existed,
had you resisted. . . .
(*AH* 12–13)

Like the tumbling of the blue-eyed Barnaby, showing off his physique before "the girls," poetry is associated with sexual "vices." Just before the conclusion, Auden seems to hear the ravens' warning:

You hope, yes,
your books will excuse you,
save you from hell:
nevertheless,
. . . .
God may reduce you
on Judgment Day
to tears of shame,
reciting by heart
the poems you would
have written, had
your life been good.
(*AH* 13)

Imagining the demons ready to carry him off to hell, Auden makes an act of obeisance, acknowledging a realm of spiritual value in which all vanities are revealed. But a printed poem is not the crypt of a monastic chapel: the Virgin may, according to the legend, appear in a statue of herself and speak, but Auden's God does not interrupt Auden's poem. In a singularly complex rhyme-scheme, Auden imagines himself confronting a performing God, a God who nevertheless reduces Auden "to tears of shame."

The past-contrary-to-fact further precludes the possibility that Auden may become Barnaby: "the poems you *would have written*, *had* your life been good" (emphasis added). Never forsaking vices and vanities in a single gesture, never "holy and humble," Auden, over and over, performs his vaults and then hears the ravens croak. Each poem stops at that spiritual edge Barnaby reaches when he determines to make penance. Even poems that do vault before the Virgin, like *New Year Letter* and "Homage to Clio," still insist on their own guilty triviality, as if poets were in perpetual need of intercession, because a verbal art, unlike a gymnastic one, can never be holy and humble. Elizabeth Mayer, in her extrapoetic world, never steps out from the niche to bless the poet.

The wish for the poetic to reach the extrapoetic, for silly, flimsy poetry to invoke a spiritual dimension where something significant might exist, dominates all of Auden's work. His central subject is the elusiveness of what is spiritually valuable, a value uneasily relegated to "outside" the work of art. This is a subject that only gradually becomes explicit in the poems themselves, as the notion of "outside" the poem emerges, and as its location changes. In his earliest work Auden voices the tentative hope that poetry can be like loving spoken words, transforming and redeeming, themselves carriers of value. Auden's later essays and poems deny art's spirituality, claiming that "Love, or truth in any serious sense" is a "reticence," the unarticulated worth that exists, if at all, outside the words on the page (" 'The Truest Poetry Is the Most Feigning' " [*SA* 44–46]).

Between these two positions, between what critics call "early" and "later" Auden, during the late 1930s and early 1940s, Auden's religious views changed. He began attending church regularly and he read widely in theology—so a merely external description of Auden's spiritual development might read. Because this change began soon after his immigration to the United States, the church whose services Auden attended was the Episcopal Church, but the "faith" was the Anglican faith in which he had been raised. Auden's return, his deliberate choice of religious belief, was gradual. There was no dramatic, clandestine second baptism, such as Eliot had, nor was there a single public announcement of his belief. Even a casual reader of Auden's book reviews in 1940 and 1941, however, could not have failed to notice the author's religious preoccupations and his theological vocabulary: eros, agape, logos, heresy, sin, grace.[3]

Auden's renewed belief may have begun emerging as early as 1937, during his trip to Spain: "On arriving in Barcelona, I found as I walked through the city that all the churches were closed and there was not a priest to be seen. To my astonishment, this discovery left me profoundly shocked and disturbed."[4] But some kind of religious attitude was present in his poetry all along; the "vision of agape" in "Out on the lawn I lie in bed" occurred in June, 1933, and the redemptive and spiritual possibilities of erotic love underlie the plot of *Paid on Both Sides*.[5] Political events provided a stimulus to this latent faith: the success of the Nazis made Auden feel that

> it was impossible any longer to believe that the values of liberal humanism were self-evident. Unless one was prepared to take a relativist view that all values are a matter of personal taste, one could hardly avoid asking the question: "If, as I am convinced, the Nazis are wrong and we are right, what is it that validates our values and invalidates theirs?"[6]

[3] See such reviews as "The Means of Grace," *New Republic* 104 (2 June 1941): 765–66, and "Eros and Agape," *Nation* 152, 26 (28 June 1941): 756–58. For Auden's own account of the change in his views, see Auden's untitled essay in *Modern Canterbury Pilgrims*, ed. James A. Pike (New York, 1956), 32–43. Carpenter's biography also has an account (273–302).

[4] Essay in *Modern Canterbury Pilgrims*, 41.

[5] For a discussion of the "vision of agape" see Edward Mendelson, *Early Auden* (New York, 1981), 159–64, 167–71.

[6] Essay in *Modern Canterbury Pilgrims*, 40.

The death of Auden's mother in 1941 gave an emotional charge to his new faith, and a crisis—now well-documented—in his relationship with Chester Kallman made faith a matter of desperate urgency.[7]

The significance for Auden's poetics was enormous. If all human activities were, as Auden came to believe, religiously grounded, no such activity (for instance, poetry) was itself expected to provide absolute truths. The notion that poetry could and ought to provide absolutes constituted the central position that Auden's poetics argued against for the rest of his life. Eliot had fought literature's appropriation of religion in the nineteenth century by having religion reappropriate culture. Auden strove to disentangle the two. Delivering the first of the T. S. Eliot Memorial Lectures in 1967, Auden said, "Mr. Eliot was a poet writing in English in the twentieth century; he was also a Christian." This double identity, according to Auden, requires an answer to the question, "What difference, if any, do my beliefs make, either to what I write, or to my conception of my vocation?" (*SW* 12). Auden's answer is a diplomatic correction of Eliot:

> The imagination is to be regarded as a natural faculty, the subject matter of which is the phenomenal world, not its Creator. For a poet brought up in a Christian society it is perfectly possible to write a poem on a Christian theme, but when he does so he is concerned with it as an aspect of a religion—that is to say, a human cultural fact, like other facts—not as a matter of faith. (*SW* 121)

In passages such as this one, Auden implicitly undoes the work of *Notes toward the Definition of Culture* (1948).

More often irreverent and iconoclastic, Auden writes against the high seriousness of the Arnolds and the Eliots:

> To a Christian . . . both art and science are secular activities, that is to say, small beer. . . . There can no more be a "Christian" art

[7] See the accounts in Carpenter's biography and in Dorothy Farnan, *Auden in Love* (New York, 1984).

> than there can be a Christian science or a Christian diet. There can only be a Christian spirit in which an artist, a scientist, works or does not work. . . . Culture is one of Caesar's things. (*DH* 456, 458)

That "small beer" is crucial to understanding the poetics of later Auden, a poetics of apology and self-deprecation, a radical undermining of poetry itself.

Such an undermining of his own art could only come from a poet whose earliest writings had, however tentatively, attributed great powers to art. When Isherwood wrote that he had to "keep a sharp eye" on Auden in their theatrical collaborations, "or down flop the characters on their knees," and observed that "another constant danger is that of choral interruptions by angel-voices," he knew that Auden was seeking some kind of spiritual exaltation through aesthetic means.[8] In the dramatic writings of the 1930s, characters flopped on their knees and angels interrupted (Isherwood was only slightly exaggerating) because Auden did want to invoke some spiritual value. He wanted something like the appearance of Hymen at the end of *As You Like It*, or Hermione's return to life at the end of *The Winter's Tale*, signalling a time of divine blessing and universal forgiveness.

Forgiveness is sought after in these works, but it proves elusive; it is the grand finale of a dramatic work that is rehearsed but never performed, the comic ending that is noticeably manqué. The characters anticipate a reconciliation they never experience. Indistinguishable from its theatrical aspects, forgiveness is associated with weddings, music, dance, ceremony, the words of the marriage service in *The Book of Common Prayer*. Its absence is an aesthetic and literary absence. It lies "outside" as if the play's fifth act had not been completed.

In the long poems Auden wrote after his move to New York, forgiveness, and indeed all spiritual significance, is ex-

[8] Christopher Isherwood, "Some Notes on Auden's Early Poetry," *New Verse* 26–27 (November 1937): 4.

plicitly dissociated from its theatrical embodiment. These poems show the scene of reconciliation, the Shakespearean comic finale always missing in the plays of the thirties, but then emphasize its artifice. They offer only what *The Sea and the Mirror* calls "feebly figurative signs" of a realm where a less artificial forgiveness exists. In the poems' final lines, guilty speakers look beyond the poetic for forgiveness and concede their need for validation from whatever of spiritual value lies outside the poem. In this act of concession, a kind of theatrical *plaudite*, the artificial struggles to address a "real" it is chary of calling anything but nonartificial. "Outside" means "not-in-this-poem," as the audience exists outside the actors, as the Virgin exists outside Barnaby.

Caliban of *The Sea and the Mirror* forms the pattern for most of the speakers in Auden's subsequent lyric poems. The naughty boy, incorrigibly stagy, guilty but charming, trivial but longing for significance, playfully performs his poem and then undermines it. In the late forties, fifties, and sixties, Auden becomes the theatrical "presenter" of his own lyric poems, his stage the printed text of the poem. The spiritual value the speaker hopes may exist somewhere (it certainly is not in this poem) can only be indicated by *praeteritio*, as, for instance, Cicero specifies the crimes of Verres he says he cannot mention. "Outside" now is a rhetorically hypothetical realm, what-I-can't-write-about.

Ultimately, all Auden can do to indicate spiritual value is to talk about his own and poetry's inabilities. Every poem becomes an apology, undermining its own significance and alluding to the value it cannot contain. Barnaby could at least tumble before a holy icon responsive to his efforts, redeeming his frivolous art. Auden's later poetry anticipates no such redemption for itself: "I dare not ask you if you bless the poets," he coyly says to Clio, "Nor do I see a reason why you should" (*HC* 6). Clio can be invoked and praised, but she will never say, "Well have you tumbled. . . ."

The poet who, at age twenty-eight, hoped art could "teach man to unlearn hatred and learn love," recognizes at age fifty-seven the source of his inspiration in naughtiness and "vices," and imagines a judgmental God "reciting by heart / The poems you would / have written, had / your life been good." Only in the imagination of an imagined deity live the poems that do not need apology.

CHAPTER ONE

Pardon and "Pardon"

> . . . few now applaud a play that ends
> with warmth and pardon the word to all,
> as, blessed, unbamboozled, the bridal pairs,
> rustic and oppidan, in a ring-dance,
> image the stars at their stately bransles. . . .
> —"City without Walls," 1969

"PARDON'S THE WORD to all," announces Shakespeare's unbamboozled Cymbeline, shedding holy tears as lovers join in an atmosphere of universal charity. The line, one of Auden's favorites, echoes through his poems and essays for years. Pardon, along with "unbamboozled," implies reconciliation: the harmony of the dancing bridal pairs comes into being when errors are corrected and faults forgiven. If only for the duration of a grand finale, the dancers mirror a heavenly order. The idealized scene of warmth and pardon recurs over the centuries, whenever "earthly things made even / Atone together"; when Count Almaviva, more unbamboozled even than Cymbeline, begs, "Contessa, perdona!" in *Le nozze di Figaro*; when Lady Catherine condescends to visit Pemberley, "in spite of that pollution which its woods had received"; or when Iolanthe's life is saved once more, because "every fairy shall die who doesn't marry a mortal."

In Auden's plays and poems also the scene recurs: as the operatic harmony of shepherds and Wise Men in *For the Time Being*; as the reconciled spirits of loggers and foreman at the Christmas dinner in *Paul Bunyan*; as the "wedding feast" of kindred spirits in *New Year Letter*. Commentary on moments of forgiveness abounds in Auden's prose, from the 1935 description of psychoanalysis as a cure founded in "the forgiveness of sins . . . confession . . . absolution" to the 1959 observation that in drama "it is impossible to distinguish between the spirit of forgiveness and the act of pardon" (*EA* 340; *DH* 200). Whether Isabella forgives Angelo, or whether Prospero forgives Antonio, are issues of some moment for Auden (*DH* 200–201, 526). Even his epigraphs tend to focus on forgiveness, in Blake's aphoristic couplet, "Mutual forgiveness of each vice / Such are the gates of Paradise," or Hannah Arendt's pronouncement, "The possible redemption from the predicament of irreversibility—of being unable to undo what one has done—is the faculty of forgiving."

Yet the voice that invokes the scene of bridal pairs in "City without Walls" is one the poem ultimately rejects. Two subsequent speakers condemn his prolix nocturnal ravings and shut him up brusquely. But what's wrong with warmth and pardon and dancing bridal pairs? Isn't this what Auden likes, precisely the way he chose to end his libretto *Delia: A Masque of Night* (1953)? Isn't this the theatrical version of what Blake and Hannah Arendt (not to mention the Christ of the Gospels) were talking about? Isn't this ultimate spiritual value?

Not quite. Longing not for genuine reconciliation but for "a *play that ends* / with warmth and pardon" (emphasis added), this voice speaks in the tones of Auden's fuddy-duddy Anglican-Edwardian persona. Tut-tutting away in the middle of the night like a fastidious uncle, he castigates audiences for their lack of taste, not their lack of charity. What he wants is a pretty play; nothing wrong with that, but his language vaguely suggests that there is something morally wrong with disliking theatrical trappings; and that if the "word" for all is warmth and pardon, if there is enough dancing in circles, if the couples make a tidy social contrast, if everything is lovely and orderly, then blessings and spiritual values must abound.

As a literary subject, forgiveness is less important to Auden than the problem of dissociating the idea of forgiveness from the idea of art; of distinguishing pardon from "pardon," the true spiritual condition from the trappings of Shakespearean comedy in which it is usually expressed: the dance, the solemn music, the formal blessings. For Auden, the subject of forgiveness is virtually inextricable from the issue of art's representation of it.

Auden has observed that *The Tempest* ends "sourly" because the pardons granted are merely official, not permeated by love and forgiveness (*DH* 526). But when he wrote his own version of the play he did not sweeten the sourness or add more warmth and pardon, turning angry Prospero into mild Cymbeline. Instead, Auden turned his "commentary" on *The Tempest*, *The Sea and the Mirror*, into a discussion of the spiritual fraudulence of aesthetic effects. Auden's Antonio, for instance, is not interested in being forgiven but in analyzing what is spurious about Prospero's accomplishments. Antonio "reads" a hypothetical post-finale scene of *The Tempest* as if it were a play pretending to genuine warmth and pardon:

> . . . it undoubtedly looks as if we
> Could take life as easily now as tales
> Write ever-after: not only are the
>
> Two heads silhouetted against the sails
> —And kissing, of course—well-built, but the lean
> Fool is quite a person, the fingernails
>
> Of the dear old butler for once quite clean,
> And the royal passengers quite as good
> As rustics, perhaps better, for they mean
>
> What they say, without, as a rustic would,
> Casting reflections on the courtly crew.
> Yes, Brother Prospero, your grouping could
>
> Not be more effective: given a few
> Incomplete objects and a nice warm day,
> What a lot a little music can do.
>
> (*CP* 360)

This is one version of that perfectly reconciled society that the nocturnal voice of "City without Walls" commends, yet to Antonio it is a "grouping," an artificial, primarily visual joining of disparate selves to create the illusion of harmony. Victims of Prospero's music, unconscious of the special effects they endure and the scene they form part of, the characters bask in a mild aesthetic glow, thinking (so Antonio implies) they are nicer than they used to be. "On the stage," writes Auden, "it is impossible to show one person forgiving another," but it is not impossible to show someone orchestrating a comic ending (*DH* 200). Auden shows more orchestration, not more forgiveness, than Shakespeare.

"What a lot a little music can do"—Auden knew that well, having confused aesthetic effect with spiritual transformation on one recent occasion. In the opening passage of *New Year Letter*, Auden describes a visit to Elizabeth Mayer on 4 September 1939, the day England entered what became the Second World War.[1] Painfully conscious of disorder in the macrocosm, Auden finds a pleasanter and more orderly little world in Elizabeth Mayer's cozy "cottage on Long Island." The manuscript draft shows Auden correcting himself about what exactly he did find there.

> . . . Buxtehude as we played
> One of his *passacaglias* made
> Our minds a *civitas* of sound
> Where nothing but assent was found,
> For love had set in order sense
> And feeling and intelligence. . . .[2]

But why "love"? Is Buxtehude a prophet of charity? The *civitas* is composed of "sound," the "assent" a musical harmony. Ever wary of the illusory spiritual exaltation inspired by music, Auden crossed out "love" and wrote in "art." To music, not agape, belongs the credit for the temporary feeling of warmth and pardon. Elizabeth Mayer and her record player may just have been Prospero and his fairy spirits.

Hence Auden begins *The Sea and the Mirror* with a warning not to confuse the poem with anything spiritually significant.

[1] England and France declared war on 3 September 1939. According to Carpenter's biography, Auden visited Elizabeth Mayer on 4 September 1939 (Carpenter, *W. H. Auden*, 275).

[2] Holograph manuscript in the Henry W. and Albert A. Berg Collection of the New York Public Library, Astor, Lenox, and Tilden Foundations.

"Well," says the Stage Manager, dismissing his own distinctions between the life onstage and the life offstage,

> . . . who in his own backyard
> Has not opened his heart to the smiling
> Secret he cannot quote?
> Which goes to show that the Bard
> Was sober when he wrote
> That this world of fact we love
> Is unsubstantial stuff:
> All the rest is silence
> On the other side of the wall;
> And the silence ripeness,
> And the ripeness all.
>
> (*CP* 352)

The notion of private release of emotion to an unknown, mysterious being suggests that God is referred to, but no such simple appellation is given this deity. He or she can only be described as extraliterary, unquotable. Shakespeare, by contrast, is eminently quotable: allusion is one way to show the difference between literary and metaphysical gods. Blending and combining lines from *Hamlet*, *King Lear*, and *The Tempest*, the Stage Manager locates ultimate spiritual value beyond quotation. Whatever "ripeness" is, it is not—like Shakespeare, or like Auden for that matter—quotable. And being extraliterary, extralinguistic, it is not in this poem.

I

In 1935 Auden approvingly gave a religious name and a religious purpose to one kind of art, "parable-art, that art which shall teach man to unlearn hatred and learn love" (*EA* 341–42). Twenty-five years later the religious vocabulary persisted, even though this time the definition was cast as a warning. In "The Virgin and the Dynamo" Auden sets up an analogy between the "verbal society" of a poem and a happily reconciled human society, only to caution against confusing the beauty of the first with the goodness of the second:

> Every beautiful poem presents an analogy to the forgiveness of sins; an analogy, not an imitation, because it is not evil intentions which are repented and pardoned but contradictory feelings which the poet surrenders to the poem in which they are reconciled. The effect of beauty, therefore, is good to the degree that . . . the possibility of regaining paradise through repentance and forgiveness is recognized. Its effect is evil to the degree that beauty is taken, not as analogous to, but identical with goodness, so that the artist regards himself or is regarded by others as God, the pleasure of beauty taken for the joy of Paradise, and the conclusion drawn that, since all is well in the work of art, all is well in history. But all is not well there. (*DH* 71)

Given the dangers of such confusion, why make the analogy in the first place? Why define art in terms of forgiveness? Because the need to relate poetry to something of ultimate spiritual value, whatever that "something" might be—forgiveness, love, warmth and pardon—impels Auden to get poetry as close as possible to these absolutes. But not too close: the association of "beautiful poem" and "forgiveness of sins" must not be understood as constituting identity.

The proximity is teasing: it establishes, or rather reaffirms, the border between the quotable and the unquotable, between literary textuality and extraliterary value. This is the one border in Auden's landscape that never goes away. All the gamekeepers and ambushes and neuroses that bar the way out of a frozen wasteland in the early poetry gradually lose their power to threaten and obstruct: their disappearance has been well charted. But as they disappear, the ontological barrier between art and whatever absolute values might exist outside it becomes more important and pronounced. Soon after Auden's move to New York, when the last geographical border is crossed, the ontological one becomes the chief subject of his poems and essays.

Much has been written on Auden's emigration and the subsequent changes in his poetry. Scholars on the eastern shores of the Atlantic, enchanted by the prophetic tones and apocalyptic vision of Auden in the thirties, tend to denigrate the poems he wrote on this side of the Atlantic.[3] I would like to suggest a new way of seeing the change in Auden, insisting at the same time on a strong continuity of interest between "English" Auden and "American" Auden.

The shift from *space* to *time* in Auden's titles has often been noted: in the late 1930s they "referred to Iceland, Spain, Dover, Oxford, Paris . . . Hongkong, China and Brussels." Soon after moving to New York, Auden "turned his attention . . . to time," writing *Another Time*, *New Year Letter*, "Spring in Wartime," "Autumn 1940," and *For the Time Being*.[4] For the significance of such a change, note what Auden himself wrote in 1932:

> The urge to write, like the urge to speak, came from man's growing sense of personal loneliness. . . . But, while speech begins with the feeling of separateness in space, of I-here-in-this-chair and you-there-in-that-chair, writing begins with the sense of separateness in time, of "I'm here to-day, but I shall be dead to-morrow, and you will be active in my place, and how can I speak to you?" (*EA* 305–6)

So long as Auden lived in England, his model for poetry was implicitly oral: poetry was conceived as speech, and its audience as listeners. And so long as the oral model existed even vestigially in Auden's mind, he retained the hope that poetry

[3] Seamus Heaney, in "Sounding Auden," *The Government of the Tongue*, regrets the "passing from Auden's poetry of an element of the uncanny, a trace of the Ralegh *frisson*, of the language's original 'chief woe, world-sorrow' " (126). In a recent review an American critic, William Pritchard, comments that the "consensus is that [Auden's] best poems were written in those 1930s when he was still the 'English Auden' " (review of *History and Value*, *New York Times*, 17 July 1988, Book Review section). Terence Brown, Department of Modern English, Trinity College, Dublin, expressed the same view to the author in conversation, July 1987. For earlier examples, see R. G. Lienhardt, "Auden's Inverted Development," *Scrutiny* 13 (September 1945): 138–42; Philip Larkin, "What's Become of Wystan?" *Spectator* 205 (15 July 1960): 104–5; Graham Hough, untitled review of *Homage to Clio*, *Listener* 64 (28 July 1960): 157–60; Jeremy Robson, "Auden's Longer Poems," *Encounter* 34 (January 1970): 73–74.

[4] Edward Mendelson, Preface to *The English Auden* (London, 1977): 19–20.

would in some way effect some kind of spiritual change in its audience. Although Auden knew perfectly well that his actual audience consisted of *readers*, he nevertheless used the language of "orality."[5]

By the late 1940s, Auden's definitions and metaphors took for granted a "literate" model of poetry. That is, Auden thought of poetry as writing and emphasized a reading audience. Although his aesthetic pronouncements from this later period occasionally credit poetry with minor spiritual transformations, most of the time Auden insists on poetry's inability to effect change in its readers.

The development from oral to literate models of poetry is gradual. Read chronologically, essays from the 1930s show only minor changes in an oral and "spatial" notion of poetry. In most of these essays Auden writes as if literature were a substitute for human contact, and the motivation to write virtually a wish for love. "Words are a bridge between a speaker and a listener," Auden observes in the 1932 essay "Writing." People write because they "feel alone, cut off from each other. . . . How can they get in touch again?" Books are written mainly "for company and creation." The model is not simply that of oral literature, ballads or ancient epic or drama: it is conversation:

> When we read a book, it is as if we were with a person. A book is not only the meaning of the words inside it; it is the person who means them. . . . When we say a book is good or bad, we mean that we feel towards it as we feel towards what we call a good or bad person. (*EA* 310)

Books "are like people, and make the same demands on us to understand and like them."

Auden emphasizes the materials of writing rather than the immediate, personal connection between two people only when he comments on the failure to communicate: "Forests

[5] Of many discussions of the issues involved in the contrast between spoken and written words, the clearest and most comprehensive remains Walter Jackson Ong's *Orality and Literacy: The Technologizing of the Word* (London and New York, 1982).

are cut down, rivers of ink absorbed, but the lust to write is still unsatisfied." The words "lust" and "unsatisfied" suggest how much Auden has in mind other frustrating forms of human contact while he discusses reading and writing. Literature's "purpose" is a very immediate social one, to "bridge the gulf between one person and another," particularly in a time when "the sense of loneliness increases." (Auden's definition of literature sounds like Donne's description of love, which "defects of loneliness controuls." In its ideal form poetry, also, "Interinanimates two soules.")

In the introduction to *The Poet's Tongue* (1935), Auden cites approvingly the definition of poetry as "memorable speech," and in elaborating describes a context that sounds like a private romantic encounter: poetry "must move our emotions or excite our intellect, for only that which is moving or exciting is memorable, and the stimulus is the audible spoken word and cadence, to which in all its power of suggestion and incantation we must surrender, as we do when talking to an intimate friend" (*EA* 327).

Here, as in the earlier essay, Auden's definition implies that poetry serves the life outside it, offering friendship to extratextual beings. But whereas earlier Auden had written that reading "is valuable when it improves our technique of living," here the gap between "reading" and "living" widens. In these well-known sentences Auden struggles over how exactly literature does affect "living":

> The propagandist, whether moral or political, complains that the writer should use his powers over words to persuade people to a particular course of action, instead of fiddling while Rome burns. But Poetry is not concerned with telling people what to do, but with extending our knowledge of good and evil, perhaps making the necessity for action more urgent and its nature more clear, but only leading us to the point where it is possible for us to make a rational and moral choice. (*EA* 329)

Having denied the simple notion that literature should sway people to a "particular course of action," having, that is, differentiated poetry from rhetoric, Auden cannot decide how, if at all, poetry affects those who read it. It is fairly easy to assert that poetry exists in a preimperative (or, as Eliot called it, "pre-political") realm. The problem comes when Auden tries to define the connection it does have—and that, for Auden, it obviously must have—to some kind of value in the world outside itself.

To say poetry extends "our knowledge of good and evil" is to make a kind of preconnection with moral value: our "knowledge" is increased. The next phrase relates that "knowledge" to some possible "action," but only tentatively: "perhaps." In the "perhaps" phrase Auden struggles to connect his own sense of the "necessity for action" with whatever it is that poetry does. But then even that tentative phrase is qualified: "but only leading us to the point where it is possible for us to make a rational and moral choice." Auden straddles the border here. Poetry sounds like a folktale guide who leads us up to the crossways but lets us decide which road to take. This process does end in a "rational and moral choice." However remotely and tentatively, poetry *makes us do something*. The end result of reading is some kind of "choice."

Auden's definition relegates poetry to a preimperative realm, yet still ends with "us," the readers, pausing over a decision. Insofar as the passage indicates Auden's strong impulse to connect poetry with moral or spiritual improvement, and his equally strong impulse not to, it resembles Jane Bennet's reluctantly judgmental comment (in *Pride and Prejudice*) in her letter to Elizabeth about the snobbish and bitchy Caroline Bingley, a sentence qualified by its protasis, by "almost," and by "appearance": "If I were not afraid of judging harshly, I should be almost tempted to say, that there is a strong appearance of duplicity in all this."

The same struggle is visible in the piece Auden wrote a few months later, "Psychology and Art To-day" (1935), an essay at whose heart is the question of "cure": how can people be made happier and better? Psychology cures people, says Auden, through "forgiveness of sins," "confession," and "absolution"—a remarkably religious set of terms for a secular procedure. Immediately after having so defined psychology's cure, Auden as if parenthetically sneaks art into the definition: "The task of psychology, or art for that matter"—are they really identical in their tasks? This "task" is curiously close to poetry's, as Auden had just defined it in the introduction to *The Poet's Tongue*: it is "not to tell people how to behave, but by drawing their attention to what the impersonal unconscious is trying to tell them, and by increasing their knowledge of good and evil, to render them better able to choose, to become increasingly morally responsible for their destiny" (*EA* 340–41).

The oral model still determines Auden's definitions: Auden implicitly relates the way poetry functions to the intimate conversations of psychoanalysis. The poet, like the Freudian analyst, "draws [people's] attention to" unconscious motivation and, in so doing, renders them "better able to choose." The task, however, is less moral and more spiritual: where the earlier essay oriented that momentous "choice" toward the public world, this one orients it toward the private individual's own "destiny."

But "Psychology and Art To-day" goes beyond that "choice" to a series of pronouncements that gradually attribute what I would call diffuse spiritual powers to art:

> You cannot tell people what to do, you can only tell them parables; and that is what art really is, particular stories of particular people and experiences, from which each according to his immediate and peculiar needs may draw his own conclusions. (*EA* 341)

Here Auden combines the discourses of all the "cures" he cares about, psychological, political, religious, and aesthetic, winding up with a definition of art that blends Freud, Marx, and Christ. The term "parable" implies that the purpose of literature is to make people better; yet because parables are "stories" they contain no explicit imperative. By the end of the essay, "parable-art" becomes the spiritually significant type of all art: "There must always be two kinds of art, escape-art, for man needs escape as he needs food and deep sleep, and parable-art, that art which shall teach man to unlearn hatred and learn love" (*EA* 341–42).

Escape-art is the art that does not lead back into "life": it just satisfies a fundamental need and disappears into the system. Parable-art looks across the border at the spiritually significant world where people love and hate, though the way it "teaches" will be determined by the reader's disposition, as each one "according to his immediate and peculiar needs may draw his own conclusions." How the poem is "applied," just how a literary work *teaches* us to "unlearn hatred and learn love," is not specified, but the spiritual context in which literature operates is clear.

The notion of poetry as a kind of intimate conversation between friend and friend, lover and lover, or patient and analyst, thoroughly disappears from Auden's aesthetic pronouncements after his move to New York. He had, after all, left behind family, friends, and native country; he had accomplished what Stephen Dedalus aimed to do, though with less fanfare. Distance from his audience was what he craved: his move, he wrote an English friend in 1939,

> has taught me the kind of writer I am, i.e. an introvert who can only develop by obeying his introversion. . . . I adore New York as it is the only city in which I find I can work and live quietly. For the first time I am leading a life which remotely approximates to the way I think I ought to live. I have never written nor read so much. (*EA* xx)

His poetics changed accordingly, assuming and allowing "introversion." Literature's value (noted Auden in 1951) lies specifically in the fact that it is *not* oral: "That is one of the wonderful things about the written word; it cannot speak until it is spoken to . . . thank God for books as an alternative to conversation."[6] In other essays, Auden refers matter-of-factly to the physical details of composition without the agony of his earlier comments on forests of paper and rivers of ink:

> Much as I loathe the typewriter, I must admit that it is a help in self-criticism. Typescript is so impersonal and hideous to look at

[6] Auden, "The World that Books Have Made," *New York Times*, 12 December 1951, Book Review section.

> that, if I type out a poem, I immediately see defects which I missed when I looked through it in manuscript. (*DH* 17)

> Never again will a poet feel so inspired, so certain of his genius, as he feels in these first days as his pencil flies across the page. . . . As he scribbles on he is beginning to get the habit of noticing metrical quantities. (*DH* 36)

Poetic composition is emphatically visual: the typescript is "hideous to look at," and the young poet appears to learn metrical quantities as much from the eye as from the ear, as "he scribbles on." And when posing to himself the question "Whom do you write for?" Auden answers with a model that has no oral residue, and reverses all the earlier notions of warm personal contact:

> Occasionally I come across a book which I feel has been written especially for me and for me only. Like a jealous lover, I don't want anybody else to hear of it. To have a million such readers, unaware of each other's existence, to be read with passion and never talked about, is the daydream, surely, of every author. (*DH* 12)

The passion here is *in the reading*; it is not what the reading substitutes for.

In these and other essays in *The Dyer's Hand* Auden continues to dissociate poetry from the grosser and more obvious kinds of causation: "Poetry is not magic. In so far as poetry, or any other of the arts, can be said to have an ulterior purpose, it is, by telling the truth, to disenchant and disintoxicate" (*DH* 27). Its powers are not spiritual—"Catharsis is properly effected, not by works of art, but by religious rites"—nor is the artistic sensibility religious: "No artist, qua artist, can understand what is meant by *God is Love* or *Thou shalt love thy neighbor* because he doesn't care whether God and men are loving or unloving" (*DH* 456). So much for the artist who teaches us to "unlearn hatred and learn love"; he is unqualified for the job. This is Auden's retraction of "Psychology and Art To-day."

Yet even when Auden creates the impression that he is denying poetry more powers than he is granting it, a spiritual, extraliterary purpose lurks in the language. The disenchantment and disintoxication make us, presumably, "better" in some psychological or emotional way. One distinction Auden loves to make in this period differentiates between the "Ariel" and "Prospero" elements in a poem: the former offers us beauty, "a verbal earthly paradise, a timeless world of pure play, which gives us delight precisely because of its contrast to our historical existence." The latter offers us truth, "some kind of revelation about our life which will show us what life is really like and free us from self-enchantment and deception" (*DH* 337). This is the "escape-art" and "parable-art" distinction in its fifties guise, and there still lurks in the definition of the second kind—the kind we know Auden writes, Prospero/parable—the hope that poetry will somehow make us better. Freeing us from self-enchantment and deception may sound less ambitious than teaching us to unlearn hatred and learn love, but if you keep in mind that Auden is saying this is what *poetry* may do you see how eager he still is to cross that border from the work of art to the life. Such an effect, freeing us from self-enchantment, would be impossible to calculate: don't any number of people spend their lives reading poetry and yet remain thoroughly self-enchanted and deceived?

In looking at Auden's aesthetic pronouncements I jumped from the 1930s to the 1950s because I wanted to show the radical shift from poetry-as-conversation to poetry-as-scribbles, typescript, silent book, and to indicate as well the continuity in Auden's ambiguously worded statements about what poetry does to its readers. These issues are most problematic in the 1940s, the time of transition between the oral model and the written. The elegy for Yeats is worth looking at here because it was written right on the cusp of this shift; what looks like ambivalence within the elegy in fact registers a change in Auden's attitudes.

The interrelationship of the sections of the elegy and the essay "The Public v. the Late Mr. William Butler Yeats" is significant in this context: what are now parts 1 and 3 of the elegy were published as the entire poem in the *New Republic* (8 March 1939). After they were written, but before they were published, Auden wrote the essay, which was published in *Partisan Review* (Spring 1939). Then in April 1939, the poem was printed in a longer version in the *London Mercury*. The following lines, the conclusion of the elegy, date from the original poem:

Follow, poet, follow right
To the bottom of the night,
With your unconstraining voice
Still persuade us to rejoice;

With the farming of a verse
Make a vineyard of the curse,
Sing of human unsuccess
In a rapture of distress;

In the deserts of the heart
Let the healing fountain start,
In the prison of his days
Teach the free man how to praise.

(*CP* 51)

The poet apostrophized here is certainly in the persuading business. The last line implies that he is also in the teaching business. Somehow, as a result of his "unconstraining voice," vineyards thrive and fountains flow in deserts. That is all very pretty, but how does it happen? Are these claims really any different, in their attribution of vague spiritual powers to poetry, from what Auden said in "Psychology and Art To-day"? Healing, teaching, and making vineyards, isn't this poet a kind of priest? The images carry the poem—possibly further than Auden, in a less rhetorical mood, thought appropriate.

Then, in the essay Auden wrote before he added a middle section to the poem, the "Counsel for the Defence" announces an uncrossable border between poetry and the rest of life:

> The case for the prosecution rests on the fallacious belief that art ever makes anything happen, whereas the honest truth, gentlemen, is that, if not a poem had been written, not a picture painted, not

a bar of music composed, the history of man would be materially unchanged. (*EA* 393)

The poet is only a "man of action" in "the field of language"—Auden takes the vocabulary associated with "life" and transfers it to "poetry." Yeats's "virtues" are only "linguistic" and will "appear ever more clearly through successive volumes." To move from an "unconstraining voice" to "volumes" is to move from an oral model—however metaphoric—to a written one; and from a poet who persuades and teaches and causes agricultural miracles to a poet whose linguistic virtues appear in printed volumes. To write, as Auden did in the new middle section of the elegy, printed after the essay, that "poetry makes nothing happen," is to paraphrase his own prose, and also to articulate the full implications of a poetry that is identified with "volumes," not with voice, with temporal distance, not spatial proximity.[7]

In the poems Auden wrote in the next few years the written paradigm continued to be associated with a poetics that examined and restricted the powers of art. *New Year Letter*'s title and genre relegate it inevitably to paper, and Auden announces flatly that "No words men write can stop the war." However, the diplomatic metaphor Auden uses a few lines later, calling his poem an "*aide-mémoire*," a "dispatch" that is "under Flying Seal," while retaining the notion of poetry as empapered, nevertheless reintroduces it tentatively into the arena of causality. As a "commentary" on *The Tempest*, *The Sea and the Mirror* is designated nondramatic, not performable, explicitly not-oral, something "written about" a play, at one remove from it. And in Caliban, *The Sea and the Mirror*'s most outrageous and brilliant character, Auden explores the

[7] For a discussion of Auden's additions to the poem, see Samuel Hynes, "Yeats and the Poets of the Thirties," in *Modern Irish Literature: Essays in Honor of William York Tindall*, ed. Raymond J. Porter and James D. Brophy (New York, 1971), 19. See also Lucy McDiarmid, "The Treason of the Clerks," in *Saving Civilization: Yeats, Eliot, and Auden between the Wars* (Cambridge and New York, 1984).

nature of the artist as oral performer and speaker of parables. To Caliban and his sermon-on-the-stage I would like now to turn.[8]

II

When Auden's speech to the graduates of Smith College in 1940 was printed in the college's alumnae magazine, the editor did not quote in full Auden's apologetic remark to the students that he was going to "preach a sermon."[9] In *New Year Letter* Auden listed among his aesthetic "crimes" that he had "Adopted what I would disown / The preacher's loose, immodest tone." When he reprinted by itself the sermon from *The Dog beneath the Skin* in the *Collected Poetry* (1945), Auden said in a note that the sermon demonstrated the "constant tendency of the spiritual life to degenerate into an aesthetic performance" (*CP* 242). The notion of the poet or artist as preacher of sermons exists implicitly in the notion of "parable-art," but it is not spelled out in "Psychology and Art To-

[8] In *SW* Auden makes several statements that appear to contradict the thesis I have just proposed. He writes, "Poetry is personal speech in its purest form. . . . It is essentially a spoken, not a written, word. One can never grasp a poem one is reading unless one hears the actual sound of the words, and its meaning is the outcome of a dialogue between the words of the poem and the response of whoever is listening to them" (113–14). What is missing from this analysis, however, is the implied setting or dramatic context that Auden tended to include in his comments during the 1930s: the conversation between analyst and patient or between lovers or between friends, or the sermon and its audience. This reader, "whoever is listening," is abstract and impersonally defined, and is clearly a *reader*. Auden says, "One can never grasp a poem one is *reading* unless one hears the actual sound of the words" (emphasis added). The "dialogue" of which the poem's meaning is an "outcome" is not a true, *oral* dialogue; it is a conversation created in the mind of the reader. The poet's part in this dialogue has occurred long ago, and the reader's "response" might take place several centuries later. What Auden means here, I believe, is that poetry is a configuration of *sounds*, and in order to take part in creating its meaning, the reader must hear the poem aloud in order to understand the original "voice" in the "dialogue." The reader, in other words, must recreate the "oral" situation artificially.

[9] Auden, "Romantic or Free?" *Smith Alumnae Quarterly* 31, no. 4 (August 1940): 353.

day." This is yet another element in the oral model of literature that shaped Auden's thinking in the 1930s. The pulpit as well as the analyst's chair is a source of oral pronouncements, one that Auden was tempted to use and, just as often, eager to renounce.

The paradigm of poetry-as-sermon reveals most acutely the conflict between the need to relate poetry to something of ultimate spiritual significance and the anxiety that poetry will be taken as, itself, spiritually significant. This is an anxiety Auden articulated by projecting it onto an anonymous, generic "he":

> The modern artist is in a dilemma. If he has beliefs, realizing that he cannot assume them in his audience, he is tempted to underline them in his work and to become a preacher of pious religious or political sermons to the faithful.[10]

In the Caliban of *The Sea and the Mirror* Auden embodied all the worst of these temptations. The sermon in *Dogskin* embodied some of them, but that was a lunatic's obsessional ranting. As a student of eighteen Auden had played Caliban in a school production of *The Tempest.* It was a role he sought out and relished, giving, so the story goes, a "remarkable performance."[11] Auden's fictional Caliban, another recreation of Shakespeare's character, also gives a remarkable performance.

Like the title *The Sea and the Mirror: A Commentary on Shakespeare's "The Tempest,"* the title and style of its final section dramatize the conflicting sets of ideas involved in oral and written models of literature. "Caliban to the Audience" implies that Caliban is addressing an audience from the stage. The notion here, as in the rest of *The Sea and the Mirror*, is that this piece occurs "after" *The Tempest.*[12] Whether Cali-

[10] Auden, "Mimesis and Allegory," *English Institute Annual 1940* (New York, 1941): 17.

[11] Carpenter, *W. H. Auden*, 41.

[12] For a fuller discussion of *The Sea and the Mirror*, see chapter 3 of this book. For comments on *The Sea and the Mirror* as a rejection of Auden's 1930s poetics, see McDiarmid, *Saving Civilization*, 87–88. For an analysis of the relation of *The Sea and the Mirror* to *The Tempest*, see Lucy McDiarmid, "Artifice and Self-Consciousness in Auden's *The Sea and the Mirror*," *Contemporary Literature* 16, no. 3 (Summer 1975): 353–77.

ban's monologue is seen as a *plaudite*, an "anti-*plaudite*," or simply a harangue, its title and its speaker's use of the vocative suggest oral delivery. But the style is hardly that of traditional rhetoric. Many, many commentators have labeled Caliban's style "Jamesian," each critic writing as if he or she were the first to make this announcement, without troubling to understand *why* Henry James's style rather than George Eliot's or Dickens's or Austen's or Pericles's would be appropriate for Caliban.[13]

The explanation, I believe, is that James's style is so notoriously, so indisputably, so definitively a *written* style. That Auden thinks of James's style this way is obvious even in his essay on James. A few short quotations from the review of James's *The American Scene* will suffice:

> . . . he seems to have visited Chicago (and not to have "liked" it). (*DH* 312)

> . . . nearer to the anonymous countryside littered with heterogeneous *dreck* . . . nearer to all the "democratic" lusts and licenses. (*DH* 323)

How after all *is* the *hypocrite lecteur* to "get" all the nuances of the Jamesian "style" without the visual contrivances of italics and inverted commas? For "yes, alas, indeed yes," it is the *lecteur* and not the *écouteur* to whom Caliban "speaks." Capital letters distinguish human babble from the "real Word," human life from "that Wholly Other Life," our amateurish efforts from the "perfected Work." Ariel's echo-song, following Caliban's effusions, is labeled a "Postscript." As Walter Jackson Ong's title so elegantly "says," "The Writer's Audience Is Always a Fiction."[14] Is there any "audience" in *The Sea*

[13] Edward Callan, in *Auden: A Carnival of Intellect* (New York and Oxford, 1983), 199, and John Fuller, *A Reader's Guide to W. H. Auden* (New York, 1970), 162, term the style of Caliban's talk "Jamesian" without explaining why. In *The Poetry of W. H. Auden: The Disenchanted Island* (New York, 1963), Monroe Spears relates the Jamesian "tone" to the first part of Caliban's talk, where "the English Muse is represented as a society matron."

[14] Walter Jackson Ong, "The Writer's Audience Is Always a Fiction," *PMLA* 90 (1975): 9–22.

and the Mirror? Insofar as there are names of Shakespearean dramatis personae and theater "techies" (Stage Manager, Prompter) there are "characters," but the audience has no role. It exists in the title and implicitly in Caliban's vocatives but it has no "speaking" part. Caliban speaks what he terms the audience's "echo" but his monologue is for all intents and purposes a soliloquy.

And just as the "audience" of the title is an audience manqué, so the soliloquy is a sermon manqué: no one is listening, no one is speaking. Yet the notions of pulpit, preacher, and parable-art dominate Caliban's tone and his "message." The "text" on which he preaches is of course *The Tempest.* He is the pastor feeding his sheep, as he rudely tells the audience:

> And now at last it is you, assorted, consorted specimens of the general popular type, the major flock who have trotted trustingly hither but found, you reproachfully baah, no grazing, that I turn to and address. (*CP* 390)

Later in his sermon Caliban defines the dramatist's purpose in biblical language:

> and, ultimately, what other aim and justification has he, what else exactly *is* the artistic gift which he is forbidden to hide, if not to make you unforgettably conscious of the ungarnished offended gap between what you so questionably are and what you are commanded without any question to become. (*CP* 400)

This is indeed "parable-art." The command to be perfect is given to Abraham: "I am the Almighty God; walk before me, and be thou perfect" (Gen. 17:1). It is also given to the multitudes by Christ: "Be ye therefore perfect, even as your Father which is in heaven is perfect" (Matt. 5:48).[15] The Colossians are so commanded by Paul and the "twelve tribes" by James (Col. 4:12; James 1:4). Caliban's words insist on the identity of art and the word of God. Like the man in Matthew's parable given one talent by his lord, the artist lives under a sacred obligation to use his "gift." The phrase "what you are com-

[15] See also *DH* 135, where Auden quotes "Be ye perfect."

manded without any question to become," with its resonant spiritual authority, makes the artist's "aim and justification" indistinguishable from that of the prophet or apostle.

Until the very end of his talk, when he undergoes a kind of religious transformation, Caliban speaks in an insulting, contemptuous, derogatory tone, as the acknowledged moral and intellectual superior of his congregation. The "message" of his sermon up to this point is consistent with poetry's purpose as Auden defines it in the essays of the 1930s. He is "leading" the members of the audience to the point where they can "make a rational and moral choice"; he is "increasing their knowledge of good and evil, to render them better able to choose, to become increasingly morally responsible for their destiny." The following summary of the "sermon" part of "Caliban to the Audience" shows that Caliban is indeed pointing out to the members of the audience the extent of their freedom, existentially speaking, and, hence, their ability to determine their destiny and their responsibility so to do.

Caliban speaks in three "roles": (1) he speaks what he calls the audience's "echo"; (2) he delivers a "special message" from Shakespeare to any future playwrights in the audience; (3) he speaks "on behalf of Ariel and myself." In each phase or role Caliban and Ariel, as a pair, define the area of life in which freedom exists. In the first role Caliban utters the notions of a naive audience that sees its own life as dominated by necessity and that desperately craves escape. For such people, art represents the only area in which choice is possible. Here, then, Caliban and Ariel are characters in a play, and represent the choices Shakespeare offers.

In the next role, Caliban delivers Shakespeare's advice to an aspiring playwright, an "apprentice in the magical art." This "strange young man" is seen as free to make decisions about his own life: he has, for instance, "decided on the conjuror's profession." Caliban and Ariel here represent aspects of that life, his imagination and his flesh, for which he is responsible. The artist has more awareness of choice than the "audience" of the first role: they made no choices whatsoever. Passively, they looked to art as a realm of freedom but did not, themselves, create. The playwright, however, must control and direct "Ariel" and "Caliban."

In the next role, Caliban addresses the audience "on behalf of Ariel and myself." Ariel and Caliban, too, have increased in power; first characters in a play, then aspects of a real life, they can now speak to the audience in their own persons, and represent alternate ways of living. What is chosen has expanded to include not merely the self but the world. Freedom is no longer the special privilege of artists; it belongs to every member of the audience. And it brings a responsibility that may be overwhelming. On the "Journey of Life," says Caliban, there are "three or four decisive instants." At each one there arises a temptation to shrink from choice, to avoid the complexities of a world whose nature is so entirely at one's own disposition. Some people may abdicate responsibility and put Caliban "in charge." Longing for a world of fleshly simplicity, they will find themselves only in "secular stagnation." Alternately those who want to live in a world beyond choice rather than before it will put Ariel in charge. Longing to be delivered from "this hell of inert and ailing matter," they create an opposite hell where "everything suggests mind," a "nightmare of public solitude."[16] Those, that is, who refuse the responsibility of their freedom end up in despair.

Caliban stops his exposition of existential freedom abruptly because, he says, he feels frustrated by his inability to effect any spiritual change in his audience. The source of this frustration lies not in any failure of his own, God forbid, but in the spiritual ineptitude of his flock:

> I have tried . . . to raise the admonitory forefinger, to ring the alarming bell, but with so little confidence of producing the right result, so certain that the open eye and attentive ear will always interpret any sight and any sound to their advantage, every rebuff as a consolation, every prohibition as a rescue . . . that I find myself

[16] For Auden's diagram and systematic explanation of these two "hells," see Kenneth Lewars, "Auden's Swarthmore Chart," *Connecticut Review* 1, no. 2 (1968): 44–56.

almost hoping, for your sake, that I have had the futile honour of addressing the blind and the deaf. (*CP* 399)

In his thwarted desire to enlighten those on the other side of the stage Caliban feels like the "dedicated dramatist,"

who, in representing to you your condition of estrangement from the truth, is doomed to fail the more he succeeds, for the more truthfully he paints the condition, the less clearly can he indicate the truth from which it is estranged, the brighter his revelation of the truth in its order, its justice, its joy, the fainter shows his picture of your actual condition. (*CP* 399)

Caliban's contempt is "the preacher's loose immodest tone," immodest because he assumes that *he* knows the truth he cannot convey to his ignorant audience, those "consorted specimens of the general popular type." Caliban has been trying to "save" his audience, and as he identifies the dramatist's purpose it is indistinguishable from that of the preacher.

But "at the very moment that irony is thought of as a knowledge able to order and to cure the world, the source of its invention runs dry."[17] Caliban now proceeds to defrock himself. In a grand act of concession that starts slowly but builds to a momentous resolution, Caliban undermines all the spiritual authority he has been flaunting. The concession begins as Caliban defines himself as an actor, instead of the "absolutely natural" being who *replaced* the "hired impersonators." To call himself an actor means more than just a playful turning inside-out of tenors and vehicles; it means Caliban acknowledges that the self who was speaking is inauthentic, fictional, contingent in being, not the authoritative, autonomous superior priest he had attempted to appear, beyond correction, beyond irony. He has been an actor in something like "the greatest grandest opera rendered by a very provincial touring company indeed."

[17] Paul de Man's analysis of E.T.A. Hoffmann's version of irony fits Caliban's talk exactly. See "The Rhetoric of Temporality" in *Blindness and Insight* (Minneapolis, 1983), 218.

> Our performance—for Ariel and I are, you know this now, just as deeply involved as any of you—which we were obliged, all of us, to go on with and sit through right to the final dissonant chord, has been so indescribably inexcusably awful . . . we floundered on from fiasco to fiasco. (*CP* 401)

Philosophically, Caliban's authority is undermined because of the artificial and dependent nature of his existence; spiritually, it is undermined because his performance was *bad*. Caliban has just become conscious, himself, of the "gap" between what he is and what he is "commanded without any question to become." His bungled performance constantly reveals its failures and vanities: he and Ariel stand "down stage with red faces and no applause."

As the buoyant self-confidence that propelled Caliban's verbosity for some twenty-nine pages fails him, Caliban slows down: "There is nothing to say. There never has been,—and our wills chuck in their hands—There is no way out. There never was." The dashes on the printed page have to stand in for long theatrical pauses, to give the impression that Caliban really does feel that there is "nothing to say." It is easy enough to see that his speech does not in fact stop at this point, that the rest of the page is not white, and that the speech even continues on to another page. How then to register this grand spiritual transformation? Caliban changes his understanding of borders:

> . . . our shame, our fear, our incorrigible staginess . . . are still, and more intensely than ever, all we have: only now it is not in spite of them but with them that we are blessed by that Wholly Other Life from which we are separated by an essential emphatic gulf of which our contrived fissures of mirror and proscenium arch—we understand them at last—are feebly figurative signs. (*CP* 402)

The border is not between preacher Caliban, wise, sophisticated, superior, and his dim-witted audience on the other side of the stage. The "essential emphatic gulf" separates Caliban the prototypical imperfect human being, shameful, afraid, incorrigibly stagy, from "that Wholly Other Life" of spiritual plenitude. The division between stage and audience is only a "feebly figurative sign" of that grander separation. The stage border from which Caliban lorded it over the audience is not a "signified" but a "signifier," not an ultimate meaning but merely a sign of some other, further meaning. Caliban's speech has not consciously "represented" human estrangement from the truth but has unconsciously embodied it.

Only now does Caliban understand his own "staginess," his childish, narcissistic pleasure in performing and showing off, in uttering the "sounds which, as born actors, we have hitherto condescended to use as an excellent vehicle for displaying our personalities and looks." This sassy, jaunty, arrogant character now purports to hear a voice other than his own that "delivers its authentic molar pardon." Caliban's vocabulary for this pardon is limited; he can conceive of its source only in aesthetic terms, as "the perfected Work which is not ours." He finally realizes that he himself is not a source of ultimate meanings, preaching the great Signified from his pulpit, but only a guilty and imperfect purveyor of signifiers.

Yet even though Caliban cannot describe any ultimate truth, he knows *what he cannot articulate*, and characterizes himself now by his inability to do more than act rather than his ability to supersede "impersonators." His is the only possible position beyond the reach of irony, the Socratic ἐγὼ δ', ὥσπερ οὖν οὐκ οἶδα, οὐδ' οἴομαι.[18] Perhaps the very fact that his speech finally does *end* constitutes itself a powerfully figurative sign of his concession.

III

The gulf between human words and the "real Word which is our only *raison d'être*" remained emphatic. Never again, after Caliban, did Auden worry about preaching, nor did he attempt any poem that could be mistaken for parable-art. In-

18 "That which I don't know, I don't think that I know." From the *Apology*, section 6D.

stead of trying to cross the border between poetry and some kind of spiritual value, Auden in his later poems plays fanfares around the barrier, trumpeting and flaunting his inability to cross over. He revels in art's inability to be anything but itself, at most a rite of praise, at least frivolity, amusement, play.

One word for the spiritual richness that poems cannot reach is "love": this was the great unmentioned in the early essay "Writing," which traced the "urge to write" to the "sense of personal loneliness." "Love" haunted all Auden's early definitions of poetry, inspiring "the audible spoken word and cadence, to which in all its power of suggestion and incantation we must surrender, as we do when talking to an intimate friend." This was the power that Auden thought had "set in order sense" that first afternoon at Elizabeth Mayer's, but that turned out instead to be "art." And "love" is the great unexpressible in Auden's later poetics, a literary subject but never an emotion "signified" by literature.

"By all means sing of love but, if you do, / Please make a rare old proper hullabaloo," begins " 'The Truest Poetry Is the Most Feigning' " (1954), but it ends by acknowledging that love *cannot* be written about: "love, or truth in any serious sense, / Like orthodoxy, is a reticence" (*SA* 44–46). When Touchstone tells Audrey that the "truest poetry is the most feigning," he means two things: that poetry is most itself when it is most artificial, most obviously "poetic"; and that this same most typical poetry comes from longing and desire. The "love" that Auden advises singing about is a literary love: quoting Shakespeare, citing Dante, writing in heroic couplets, Auden openly advises literary artifice: "Be subtle, various, ornamental, clever."

The model of poetry in " 'The Truest Poetry Is the Most Feigning' " is obviously not oral; how but through the printed word does any twentieth-century person know Dante and Shakespeare's poetry? Auden is explicit about the physical material of poetry making, and the distance of poetry writing from conversation with "an intimate friend": "Stick at your desk and hold your panic in," he advises the poet living in the midst of political turmoil, and he warns the young poet about readers' reactions:

> Though honest Iagos, true to form, will write
> *Shame!* in your margins, *Toady! Hypocrite!*,
> True hearts, clear heads will hear the note of glory
> And put inverted commas round the story,
> Thinking—*Old Sly-boots! We shall never know*
> *Her name or nature. Well, it's better so.*
>
> (*SA* 46)

Given the possible readers' possible marginal comments, the political/aesthetic argument is played out entirely in writing, some of it even unread by its implied audience (e.g., "*Shame!*" and "*Toady! Hypocrite!*"). This is a poetry that has nothing to do with the "audible spoken word" and its intimate, suggestive cadences: this is a poetry of desks and margins and " '!' ".

The very border that Auden announces poetry cannot cross, the way to "love, or truth in any serious sense," is indicated typographically:

> You're so in love that one hour seems like two,
> But write—*As I sat waiting for her call,*
> *Each second longer darker seemed than all*
> (Something like this but more elaborate still)
> *Those raining centuries it took to fill*
> *That quarry . . .*
>
> (*SA* 44)

and so on and so forth. The difference in status between what is italicized and what is not mirrors the difference between the poem and the feelings that inspired it, the "feigning" (artifice) and the "feigning" (desire). The notion of inauthenticity is built into poetry. It forms, however unconsciously, a fundamental part of any reasonably sophisticated reader's expectation. That is what Eliot meant when he wrote that "Poetry is not an expression of emotion; poetry is an escape from emotion." Anything on paper that looks like a poem and is printed and published as such becomes automatically, willy-nilly, a part of literary tradition. However genuine the love that inspired the poem may be, once it is in print it becomes "love." Once W. H. Auden publishes a poem, it has more in common, ontologically, with a Shakespearean sonnet than with the real feelings of WHA.

Poetry that flaunts its typographic features implicitly acknowledges its status as play. Here Auden explains the rules of the game; " 'The Truest Poetry Is the Most Feigning' " is a how-to poem. Just as badminton is played with birdies and checkers with wooden disks, so poetry is played with words, *O Happy Grief* or *lily-breasted* or *lion-chested*. Precisely because this game is verbal, there exists always the special danger of confusing its deliberate inauthenticity with the verbal expression of authentic feelings. And these "authentic feelings" get into the poem only when Auden insists on poetry's inability to talk about them: "No metaphor, remember, can express / A real historical unhappiness."

The end of " 'The Truest Poetry Is the Most Feigning,' " like the end of Caliban's speech, pays a kind of homage to the love that inevitably lies outside poetry. I say "a kind of" homage because, since this *is* a poem, it really does not have the vocabulary to cope with what is outside itself: it cannot express a "real historical" anything. And so just as Caliban can only indicate the failure of his own performance and the inadequacy of his words, just as the Stage Manager identifies ripeness with silence, so Auden here can only suggest that what is genuine is not expressed: ". . . love, or truth in any serious sense, / Like orthodoxy, is a reticence."

And the poem has to end on that note. The frivolity and insignificance of poetry have been amply demonstrated; having introduced the possibility of a "serious" love, Auden can do no more than acknowledge its existence somewhere off the page. To talk about it more would be to turn it into a typographic game like the other kind of love he has talked about: the word "reticence" must end the poem, because to say more would be unreticent.

Because poetry turns "authentic" feelings into "inauthentic" feigning, even a proper name that is recognizably unique becomes the name of a literary character once it is part of a line of poetry. Of Shakespeare's Sonnet 57, "Being your slave," Auden once asked, "Can you imagine showing it to the person you were thinking of? Vice versa, what on earth would you feel, supposing someone you knew handed you the sonnet and said: 'This is about you'?" (*FA* 104). The border between the beloved object, a unique historical being, and the subject of the poem, between the personal and the literary uses of the proper name, inspired the later Auden's prose and poems alike. The border is particularly problematic when the beloved object is a deity:

> Poems, like many of Donne's and Hopkins's, which express a poet's personal feelings of religious devotion or penitence, make me uneasy. It is quite in order that a poet should write a sonnet expressing his devotion to Miss Smith because the poet, Miss Smith, and all his readers know perfectly well that, had he chanced to fall in love with Miss Jones instead, his feelings would be exactly the same. But if he writes a sonnet expressing his devotion to Christ, the important point, surely, is that his devotion is felt for Christ and not for, say, Buddha or Mahomet, and this point cannot be made in poetry; the Proper Name proves nothing. (*DH* 458)

Even a deity becomes a literary figure of the same status as Orlando and Rosalind once he or she is apostrophized. Donne's "Hymn to Christ" and "Hymn to God, My God" have arguably little to do with Jesus Christ. The evident artifice of such poems emphasizes the literariness of the beings they address: Donne's "Eternall root / Of true Love" and Herbert's "My God, My King" have as much in common with each other as either does with the oracle delivered of great Apollo's priest in the third act of *The Winter's Tale.*

In "Dichtung und Wahrheit (An Unwritten Poem)" (1961) Auden argues with philosophical fastidiousness the issues he had discussed with cavalier confidence in " 'The Truest Poetry Is the Most Feigning.' " Not the poet assuring other poets of poetry's triviality and artifice, he adopts the role of a lover trying to write poetry in an authentic voice about an authentic, beloved You; a lover trying to cross the barrier between love and "love." Like the title of the earlier poem, this one is a literary allusion, and emphasizes the separability and separateness of "poetry" and "truth." How can something in print be "(An Unwritten Poem)"? Because it is in *prose*, as if Auden wants to imply, this is *prepoetic*, what never got out of prose into poetry; as if "Dichtung und Wahrheit" exists somewhere between the feelings of the actual, historical W. H. Auden, and the poem he would have written out of those feelings, between "Wahrheit" and "Dichtung." The poem itself *is* the border. It exists because "Dichtung" and "Wahrheit" cannot be the same. Like the wastelands and orchards of Auden's earliest poems, they simply do not meet; there is no path between them. Poetry looking over at what it thinks is spiritual significance is simply poetry looking at itself mimicking the truth. All this prose, looking back to the "feelings" and forward to the unwritten poem, advertises the philosophical border between signified and signifier, though it can only talk about two signifiers.

And, given the impenetrability of the border, the literary work is inevitably empapered, with typography creating ontological distinctions:

> Expecting your arrival tomorrow, I find myself thinking *I love You*: then comes the thought—*I should like to write a poem which would express exactly what I mean when I think these words.* (*HC* 35)

The italics here represent the genuine feelings of the prepoetic state, the unitalicized lines the border from which Auden surveys both "Wahrheit" and "Dichtung." Auden has to use a different typographic sign to indicate the unwritten poem:

> . . . the truth of this poem must be self-evident. It would have to be written, for example, in such a way that no reader could misread *I love You* as "I love you." (*HC* 35–36)

"Wahrheit" is italicized, "Dichtung" in inverted commas. And the author of the "unwritten poem," whose philosophical analysis exists in unadorned typeface, purports to discover the impossibility of connecting them.

How, then, to write a love poem in which the personal, unique individuals I and You do not become fictitious characters but remain "persons whose existence and histories could be verified by a private detective"? It cannot be done. As if by a chemical reaction, the moment the feelings hit the page they become false: embodied in ink, they *become* feigning, fictitious, *littérature*. "So," announces Auden at the end, "this poem will remain unwritten. That doesn't matter. Tomorrow You will be arriving."

"Dichtung und Wahrheit" leaves unaddressed the problem of what kind of relation prose has to "Wahrheit." Is the "I" of "Dichtung und Wahrheit" W. H. Auden? Is the "You" Chester Kallman? Doesn't prose create fictitious characters just as poetry does? Or can the kind of prose in which philosophical discourse occurs stand apart from these distinctions? The issue does not arise here because "Dichtung und Wahrheit" is not about feelings, or about something Auden would call spiritually significant: it is about an aesthetic poser, the power of what is *written* to transform truth into falsehood, the extrapoetic into the poetic.

Both in his early conception of poetry as oral and in his later conception of poetry as written, Auden is not alone among twentieth-century poets. Less ambivalently than Auden, Yeats and Eliot praised the model of a small, homogeneous community whose bards uttered the people's own shared values. As the comedienne Marie Lloyd or the ancient Irish *fili*, such figures spoke without mediation to an audience of the like-minded, never needing to convert or change or improve, never needing to create vineyards and fountains. But for modern poets, who did not live among the like-minded, the idea of speaking poetry to an audience was hard to distinguish from preaching, with all the attendant dangers Auden dramatizes in Caliban. The oral model seemed useful on the small scale, but ultimately Auden came to feel that writing poetry was not in fact like having a conversation with a friend or an analysand. It was more like having a "million . . . readers, unaware of each other's existence."[19]

Other modern poets have played with the visual and typographic possibilities of a poetry that is emphatically not-oral. Such playfulness is a trademark of e. e. cummings, who inherited it from French poets in the tradition of Rimbaud. John Hollander wrote emblem poems (one shaped like a bottle of burgundy, another like an hourglass) in the tradition of George Herbert.[20] But so far as I know Auden is the only poet for whom italics and quotation marks leap up and bar the way between poetry and forgiveness or love.

Abandoning the oral model of poetry meant, for Auden, acknowledging the inevitable inauthenticity of poetry. A game played with marks on a page could not be the intimate conversation of friends. Even as he dramatizes the inauthenticity, in a poem like " 'The Truest Poetry Is the Most Feigning,' " Auden lets a little sadness in. Love, "or truth in any serious sense," is forever barred from the poem. Clio is a muse of "merciful silence" who does not read poetry. In *The Sea and the Mirror*, in "Homage to Clio," and in so many of his later poems, Auden's relegation of value to silence rather than to blankness signifies a vestige of the oral model, a last bit of belief in sound, rather than surface, as a carrier of the spirit.

[19] For the shift from oral to written models in the case of three modern poets, see McDiarmid, "The Living Voice in the Thirties," in *Saving Civilization.*

[20] See "For a Thirtieth Birthday, with a Bottle of Burgundy" and "The Shape of Time" in John Hollander, *Movie-Going and Other Poems* (New York, 1962), 37, 38.

CHAPTER TWO

The Generous Hour: Poems and Plays of the 1930s

Then shall they give their troth to each other in this manner. The Minister, receiving the Woman at her father's or friend's hands, shall cause the Man with his right hand to take the Woman by her right hand, and to say after him as followeth.

I *N.* take thee *N.* to my wedded Wife, to have and to hold from this day forward, for better for worse, for richer for poorer, in sickness and in health, to love and to cherish, till death us do part, according to God's holy ordinance; and thereto I plight thee my troth.

Then shall they loose their hands; and the Woman with her right hand taking the Man by his right hand, shall likewise say after the Minister,

I *N.* take thee *N.* to my wedded Husband, to have and to hold from this day forward, for better for worse, for richer for poorer, in sickness and in health, to love and to cherish, till death us do part, according to God's holy ordinance; and thereto I give thee my troth.

—"The Form of Solemnization of Matrimony," *The Book of Common Prayer*

FATHER CHRISTMAS and Freud, kind grandfatherly figures with beards, benevolent, generous, and authoritative, precipitate weddings. They are sources of spiritual influx: both patriarchs liberate an erotic drive that develops into a love with redemptive powers. In *Paid on Both Sides* (1928) Father

Christmas presides over the dream that reveals the frozen, imprisoned "Man-Woman," embodiment of all sexual forces, and Freud (of "In Memory of Sigmund Freud," 1939) releases the "household of Impulse." John Nower's dream ends with a ritual that reconciles the "Accuser" and "Accused," who then "plant a tree" together (*CLP* 25). Freud, also working at the level of dream, similarly reconciles antagonistic parts of the self: he unites the "unequal moieties fractured / By our own well meaning sense of justice" (*AT* 105). These internal reconciliations have immediate social consequences: Nower wakes from his dream to propose to Anne Shaw, whose family has been feuding with his for years. In the "Occasional Poems" of *Another Time* the elegy for Freud is followed immediately by the epithalamion for Elizabeth Mann and Giuseppe Antonio Borgese, of whose wedding Auden writes,

> Yet the seed becomes the tree;
> Happier savants may decide
> That this quiet wedding of
> A Borgese and a Mann
> Planted human unity. . . .
>
> (*AT* 107)

From 1928 through 1939, this was Auden's paradigmatic ritual: a wedding that reconciles a divided, unhappy community, regenerating its natural life and redeeming its spirit.

Throughout the thirties the vision of bridal pairs in a blessed, forgiven community haunted Auden's imagination. Freud and Father Christmas remain in the background: Auden's earliest plays and poems place on married love the burden of redeeming the world. Engaged couples have the responsibility of secular saviors; they are expected to cure their doomed societies, performing the rites of forgiveness that everyone else is unable to enact. In the longer early works—*Paid on Both Sides*, *The Dance of Death* (1933), *The Dog beneath the Skin* (1935), and *On the Frontier* (1938)—the characters see themselves as actors in a play that must conclude with a traditional comic ending. All spiritual significance is situated in the theatrical grand finale that everyone looks forward to, a spectacular ceremony that indicates the presence of "warmth and pardon" for all. Through the diffuse, beneficent effect of much music, song, and dance, all the separate, eccentric, alienated members of the community will be conjoined, their lives exalted in the intensity of ritual.

This is the "ending" they anticipate: but they are invariably disappointed. In most of the poems and plays Auden wrote through *On the Frontier* (1938), weddings appear only in ceremonial bits and pieces—some brideless bridegrooms, fragments of nuptial vows, a few bars of Mendelssohn or *Lohengrin*—and lovers fail to save. The incomplete wedding seems as much a theatrical failure as a spiritual one. The script is the Form of Solemnization of Matrimony from the *Book of Common Prayer*, the actors the bride and groom, the audience wedding guests. The community's reconciliation depends on the completed production of a play present in anticipation, in rehearsal, and in musical and literary fragments. This play is cut short, its resolution thwarted, people's expectations betrayed. The spiritual value it promised proves elusive, as if the fifth act of a comedy had been abruptly denied performance but remained to haunt and disturb the imagination.

I

Only in one early poem, the recently published "Epithalamion for the wedding of Iris Snodgrass and Alan Sinkinson" (1931), does the wedding appear in unfragmented form.[1] As an occasional poem celebrating the marriage of real people, the epithalamion had of necessity to fulfill everyone's happiest expectations. It places the bride and groom at the center of natural, social, and spiritual worlds, and attributes to them a generalized redemptive power to satisfy eros and inspire agape. This epithalamion provides the only example from the 1930s of the

[1] See appendix to Lucy McDiarmid, "Auden's 1931 Epithalamion and Other Generous Hours," *Modern Language Quarterly* 46, no. 4 (December 1985): 407–28. The epithalamion is also printed in W. H. Auden and Christopher Isherwood, *Plays, and Other Dramatic Writings, by W. H. Auden, 1928–1938*, ed. Edward Mendelson (Princeton, 1988), 484–87.

way Auden's paradigm works ideally, a ceremonial occasion that creates, in the wonderful phrase of the poem, a "generous hour."

The 1931 epithalamion may be modeled to some extent on Spenser's "Epithalamion," although the conventions Auden observes are typical of most Renaissance epithalamia.[2] The refrain that follows each stanza ("Fill up the glasses with champagne and drink again") is the most obvious connection, possibly inspired by Spenser's variations on "That all the woods may answer, and your eccho ring" and his command, "Poure out the wine without restraint or stay." Moreover, Auden's poem, like Spenser's, moves from morning to night, from "To-day these new ones are beginning to be one" and "Lord, be here to-day" through "We are all here now" to "day is almost done." Just as Spenser, near the beginning, invokes the local Irish "nymphes of Mulla," Auden begins with a reference to the "Clydeside dockyard" (Alan Sinkinson was a colleague at Larchfield Academy, near Glasgow on the Firth of Clyde). And Auden closes with a wish for safety from supernatural evils, as Spenser, toward the end of "Epithalamion," asks for safety from "the Pouke" and "other evill sprights."

The traditional formality of the epithalamion coincides perfectly with Auden's interest in the ceremonial and theatrical. As speaker of the poem, he is also "Presenter" of the ritual's performers. He summons the guests with their wedding presents ("Let all bring gifts with them these have invite [sic]"), names them, and directs the bride and groom: "Approach now, Alan," "Receive him, Iris." From the first stanza's charged sexual implications through the last stanza's allusion to grander natural energies, the bride and groom are imagined as emanating a powerful life force. The opening reference to the liner's "maiden voyage" introduces the motif of champagne and also suggests, even in the first stanza, the intercourse with which the day will end: the liner is seen "sliding

[2] The best discussion of the conventions of Renaissance epithalamia is Thomas M. Greene, "Spenser and the Epithalamic Convention," in *The Prince of Poets: Essays on Edmund Spenser*, ed. J. R. Elliott, Jr. (New York, 1968), 152–69.

over the greased / Slipway, displacing the water she touched / For the first time." Even the "Lord" whose presence is requested is an erotic god whose blessing encourages proper development of sexuality. He makes "the virgin to leave her door unlocked" and pleases "the daughter sitting on her father's knee," but makes her leave it so her desires may be more appropriately directed to a husband. The source of all natural energy, he brings "the swallows past the Scillies" and looses the "urgent pollen" to "find the pistil, force its burglar's entry."

Alan and Iris are also the focus of social activity. A centripetal force, the couple has drawn together disparate, eccentric, far-flung individuals:

> We are all here now, Mildred the religious Aunt,
> Thomas the groomsman, Nat the confidant,
> Morgan the Welsh cousin; representatives
> Of all the gods who have controlled the lives,
> The drugged Princess, and the jerseyed lighthousekeeper
> We come, some more, some less, but all to honour[3]

Alan Sinkinson's best man was Thomas Phillips; one of Iris Snodgrass's bridesmaids was Natalie Gold. The rest of the people, according to Mrs. Sinkinson and her brother Arnold Snodgrass, a good friend of Auden's, were Auden's inventions.[4]

At this point in a more classical epithalamion the poet would describe the religious ceremony. He has described the village and the natural context, invoked the presence of god and assembled the wedding guests. But it is just here that Auden is untraditional, and most original. The following three stanzas (stanzas 8–10) are the most inspired in the poem, and were used in their entirety in *The Dog beneath the Skin*. Here, Auden leaves the ceremonial events of the wedding and sees the marriage in terms of its effect on a world in bondage, char-

[3] See appendix to McDiarmid, "Auden's 1931 Epithalamion," 426.
[4] Letter from Iris Sinkinson to Lucy McDiarmid, 4 June 1985.

acterized chiefly by a frustrated impulse to love. The "performance" of the rite by bride and groom releases the force of love:

It's not this only we praise, it's the general love
Let cat's mew rise to a scream on the tool-shed roof
Let son come home to-night to his anxious mother
Let vicar lead choir-boy into a dark corner
Orchid flower to-day, that flowers every hundred years,
Boots and slavey be found dutch-kissing on stairs

Fill up the glasses with champagne and drink again

Let this be kept as a generous hour by all,
This once let uncle pay for nephew's bill
Let nervous lady's gaucheness at tea-time be forgiven
Let thief's explanation of theft be taken;
And fag caught smoking shall escape his usual beating
To-night the expensive whore shall give herself for nothing

Fill up the glasses with champagne and drink again

Yes, the land-locked state shall get its port to-day,
The midnight worker in laboratory by sea
Shall find beneath cross-wires that he looks for
Tonight asthmatic clerk shall dream of boxer;
Let cold hearts wish be granted, desire for a desire
Give to coward now his hour of power

Fill up the glasses with champagne and drink again. . . . [5]

In the first of these stanzas, the exhortation "Let" implies a connection between "this," the love of Alan and Iris, and "the general love," all manifestations of sexual impulse: animal, oedipal, pederastic, floral, menial. The charm of Auden's list is its indiscriminate, nonjudgmental inclusion of neurotic, rarefied, forbidden, and furtive desires. Through "this" love, all natural impulse is freed from restriction.

The following stanza adds to the release of sexual energy

[5] See appendix to McDiarmid, "Auden's 1931 Epithalamion," 427.

the notion of charity. The marriage can inspire more than the mere satisfaction of drives or selfish needs; it can inspire generosity. Auden's examples here mix issues of social behavior with resonant religious paradigms. The nervous lady's gaucheness might exist in Barbara Pym's world, but her awkwardness is nevertheless a fault to be "forgiven." The later examples suggest a Christ-like forgiveness of sinners, the thief and the disobedient boy: pardon is the word to all. The final example is virtually the apocalyptic version of the first: for the uncle, this once, to pay his nephew's bill is "generous" in a limited financial way, but for the "expensive whore" to give herself for nothing is the ne plus ultra of generosity, transforming other people's eros into her own agape. The joining of criminal types with spiritual transformations anticipates Herod's soliloquy in *For the Time Being*, where he lists with horror the results of the incarnation of God in Christ:

> Justice will be replaced by pity. . . . The New Aristocracy will consist exclusively of hermits, bums, and permanent invalids. The Rough Diamond, the Consumptive Whore, the bandit who is good to his mother . . . will be the heroes and heroines of the New Tragedy. (*CP* 459)

The changes wrought by a religious savior in 1944 are the same as those wrought by married love in 1931.

In the third of these stanzas, Auden moves beyond the optative "let" to the assertive "shall." The poem accumulates intensity, claiming rather than wishing for the results of the marriage. These examples suggest even greater liberation from the prison Auden later described in the phrase "each in the cell of himself." The idea of a landlocked state's getting a port suggests a miraculous breakthrough from centuries of imprisonment; the image of suddenly opening onto water recalls the first stanza's liner on her maiden voyage "Trailing the folding furrow over the long sea" but goes beyond its more limited sexual implications to a sense both of long-deserved release and of reward. Almost like Keats's stout Cortez, the landlocked state suddenly experiences the gift of a seemingly boundless world. This stanza moves beyond charity to grace:

it lists not personal transformations but wondrous gifts. The midnight worker's hours of toil and frustration are over; he has been working in a laboratory "by the sea," at the edge of discovery, and, today, finds "that he looks for," whatever it is that will fulfill him. The sickly clerk dreams of his ideal self; and, in the final manifestation of grace, the heart is enabled to feel.

Like a traditional epithalamion, Auden's follows the lovers to bed. Superhuman figures, inspiring sexual fulfillment and reconciliation, they are identified with larger universal forces:

> As trees are alive in the forest and do not fall
> Sustained every day by their unconscious columnar will;
> It shall outlast the tiger his swift motions,
> Its slowness time the heartbeat of nervous nations[6]

The living forces that hold trees up are the same as those that "find the pistil" and "force its burglar's entry," but on a grander scale, as the uncultivated "forest" is more mysterious than the village and flowers referred to earlier. The married love Auden describes here is part of the sustaining force of the cosmos, more enduring than the tiger in spite of his swiftness, and a soothing power for secular anxiety.

II

The 1931 epithalamion shows in its ideal form the effect of the Solemnization of Matrimony on its unredeemed audience. Scattered metaphors and allusions to marriage in Auden's earliest poetry also associate it with the redemption of a world in bondage, but these are fragmentary and uncertain in effect. In the final section of "It was Easter as I walked in the public gardens" (1929) appears the first of several "bridegrooms," liminal figures existing tenuously at the border between unredeemed and redeemed worlds. Love, says Auden in the apocalyptic culmination of the poem, needs the "Death of the old gang," whose members include

[6] See appendix to McDiarmid, "Auden's 1931 Epithalamion," 428.

> The hard bitch and the riding-master
> Stiff underground; deep in clear lake
> The lolling bridegroom, beautiful, there.
>
> (*EA* 40)

The hard bitch and the riding-master sound like the trappings of a moribund aristocracy. But the next figure, though listed in grammatical apposition, sounds neither "hard" nor "stiff." He is "deep in clear lake," perfectly visible; he is "lolling," as if voluntarily reclining and lounging, with a kind of sensual pleasure in the water. That he is a "bridegroom" and "beautiful" adds to the impression of sensuality. His may be the degenerate beauty of an effete race, and his lolling a passivity indistinguishable from the floating of a drowned body, but because he is a bridegroom, and because the lake is clear, he sounds like the possible source of new life after the death of the old gang. For "love," according to this passage, "Needs more than the admiring excitement of union." Is the bridegroom associated with sexual union and its *narcissisme à deux*? Or is he part of the "more"? When a "bridegroom" appears without a bride, it is hard to ignore the biblical resonance: "But the days will come, when the bridegroom shall be taken from thee" (Matt. 9:15–16; see also Mark 2:19–20 and Luke 5:34–35).

The bridegroom, again without the bride, is also a potential savior in a list of three figures associated with a new dispensation in the sonnet "Just as his dream foretold" (1934). Uncertain of his own role as redeemer in relation to the people he has just met, the speaker questions, "Were they or he / The physician, bridegroom, and incendiary?" (*EA* 148). The physician may be identified with the poem's tall professor in tweed, and the incendiary with the "smiling grimy boy," but there is no figure who could be the bridegroom.[7] Unheralded in the poem, the bridegroom is another liminal figure, placed in the list between healer (physician) and destroyer (incendiary). Like the lolling bridegroom, he is found in a space be-

[7] For a discussion of this sonnet see Mendelson, *Early Auden*, 247–48.

tween old and new societies, a secular version of the Christ of the parables.

In the poems the word "bridegroom," with its religious connotations, evokes vaguely the possibility of a certain kind of salvation. In the plays, an entire ceremony rather than an isolated word tempts with the promise of a glorious reconciliation. A redemptive marriage, as aesthetically satisfying as the one in the epithalamion for Alan and Iris, persists as a finale manqué in Auden's early dramatic works. The recurrent presence of thwarted nuptials and ceremonial fragments makes the "bridal pairs," the dance, and the universal pardon conspicuous by their absence. In the collective mind of each play's community lives the expectation of a marriage that will satisfy desire, inspire generosity, and provide spiritual uplift, but the young lovers are always defined chiefly by their failure to "save."

To use the language of the 1931 epithalamion, the world of *Paid on Both Sides* is that of the "landlocked state," but it does not get its port. When John Nower and Anne Shaw become engaged, Aaron Shaw comments,

> Now this shall end with marriage as it ought:
> Love turns the wind, brings up the salt smell,
> Shadow of gulls on the road to the sea.
>
> (*CLP* 28)

Shaw's "this" ambiguously indicates both the feud and the "charade" *Paid on Both Sides*: the spiritual "ought" and the aesthetic "ought" are the same. As a resident of Nattrass and as a character in a drama, Aaron Shaw passively depends on bride and groom to reconcile the forces in his world and provide an "ending."

The wedding guests celebrate the marriage with all the appropriate paraphernalia. Handing the bride a bouquet, the "Chief Guest" recites a brief epithalamion:

> With gift in hand we come
> From every neighbour farm
> To celebrate in wine

> The certain union of
> A woman and a man;
> . . . .
> Now hate is swallowed down,
> All anger put away. . . .
>
> (*CLP* 32)

The expectations of an entire society are placed on the young lovers to make this a "generous hour." Here the dancing "bridal pairs" make their first appearance in Auden's poetry, promising a "play that ends / with warmth and pardon." The assembled families celebrate the union with a party, a poem, dance, music, and wedding feast, anticipating the reconciliation wrought by Anne and John. But the appurtenances are all it gets. Mother Shaw has not swallowed her hatred, and she persuades Seth to kill John Nower.

When the curtain reveals Anne with John's body, she speaks as if the thwarting of the marriage signified the culmination of a narrative, as if she herself were part of a "story":

> Now we have seen the story to its end.
> . . . .
> I had seen joy
> Received and given, upon both sides, for years.
> Now not.
>
> (*CLP* 33–34)

The past contrary-to-fact mood of the verb shows the ending that should have been. Like her cousin Aaron, Anne had a certain aesthetic model in mind that defined the shape of the story within which her life took place. John Nower's death provides closure—Anne speaks as if the story was definitely over—even as it forces the characters to redefine the nature of their story.

In *The Dance of Death* there is no indication anywhere that the play "ought" to end in marriage; there are no romantic trappings, no young lovers, no epithalamia and dancing couples, not even any nuptial metaphors. Yet the play ends with an ironic fragment of a wedding. The dancer of the title, an apparently "vital young man" whose frenzied activity is identified explicitly with bourgeois society's death wish, fulfills his inevitable function by dying. At that point Karl Marx enters "with two young communists" and the chorus greets him by singing a few lines "to Mendelssohn's Wedding March."[8]

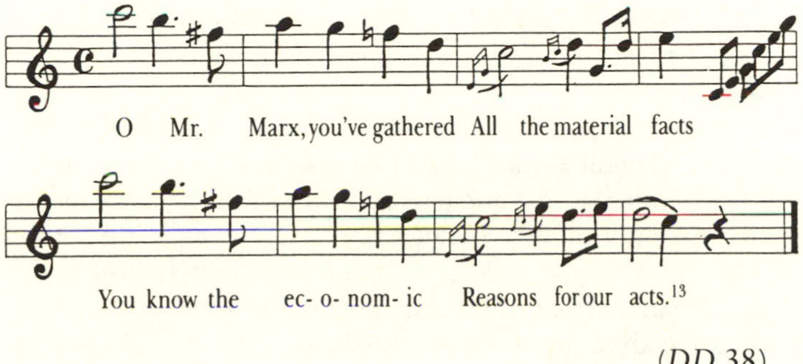

(*DD* 38)

Desperately eager to find a savior, the chorus treats Marx as bridegroom. Its members seem unaware that what their words acknowledge so cheerfully ("You know the economic / Reasons for our acts") is a form of determinism that predicts their death. As Marx diagnoses the cause of the dancer's death ("The instruments of production have been too much for him") the marriage ceremony turns into a funeral, and all exit to a dead march. Karl Marx, so announced, functions like all the other bridegrooms; he is a liminal figure whose presence clearly marks the death of a society but does not yet herald its resurrection.

The wedding march, chorus, and dramatic entrance of Marx make a grand finale that no one anticipated: unlike *Paid on Both Sides*, *The Dance of Death* has a wedding ceremony without the expectation of it. The apparent lack of connection between the resolution and the rest of the play forces one to reread the play and see what in it could have required a nuptial finale. The members of the chorus, like the family members in

[8] I would like to thank Peter Taney for copying the music.

Paid on Both Sides, passively expect someone else to enact their redemption—a hero, a leader, a demagogue, a dancer. It is they who make Marx's entrance into a ritual. The notion of a comic ending as something the characters require of the play is even more pronounced here than in *Paid on Both Sides*, because the form created by the chorus's musical outburst is so inappropriate to the situation. The absence of a bride and the death of the dancer only reveal the characters' desperation as merely theatrical, and the music and song festivities with no raison d'être.

Conceived in part in Auden's nuptial tradition, *The Dog beneath the Skin* takes the first names of its engaged couple from the 1931 epithalamion and uses several of the best stanzas late in the play. But the borrowings are used ironically: this Alan and Iris are engaged by lottery, and Iris ultimately breaks the engagement. Furthermore, the stanzas are used not to celebrate a wedding or even a serious love, but a one-night fling Alan has with a mannequin.

The idea of a marriage is introduced as a reward for a bridegroom-savior. The society of Pressan-Ambo is also under a curse. Like Sicily in *The Winter's Tale*, it will live "without an heir, if what is lost be not found." The son of Sir Bingham Crewe, the feudal lord of the region, disappeared after a quarrel with his father, and Sir Bingham's will has established an annual search for his lost heir Francis:

> Each year, his villages in turn
> Should choose by lottery a man
> To find Sir Francis if he can;
> Further, he promised half his land
> And Iris his daughter adds her hand
> In marriage to the lucky one
> Who comes home with his only son.
>
> (*DBS* 23)

Thus the whole play looks forward to the wedding on which the villages' future depends. The discovery of Francis will inaugurate forgiveness between generations, ensure continuity for the villages, and be celebrated by his sister's wedding. Before Pressan-Ambo's man is chosen this year, Iris makes her annual fill-in-the-blank vow:

VICAR. Iris Crewe, are you willing now
In the presence of these people to make your vow?
IRIS. I am.
VICAR. [IRIS *repeats each phrase after him.*]
I, Iris Crewe, do solemnly swear
In the presence of these people here,
That I will be the wedded wife
To love and cherish all my life
Of him, whoever he may be,
Who brings my brother back to me.

(*DBS* 24–25)

The essence of a marriage vow, it seems needless to say, is that two people vow to love each other. The proper name of each is written into the ceremony in *The Book of Common Prayer*: "I *N*. take thee *N*. . . ." In this travesty, *one* person vows to love "him, whoever he may be." Iris repeats her lines in the script, rehearsing the role her dead father has assigned her to perform. The absence of proper names dramatizes the overriding importance of the ceremonial element, in which alone—so the members of this society appear to believe—spiritual value inheres.[9]

A second ceremony follows to entertain the villagers in their state of dependent passivity. The nameless bridegroom, the young man who will save Pressan-Ambo by finding its lost heir, is chosen by lot in a manner similarly arbitrary. The vicar, his eyes blindfolded, chooses the name out of a hat:

[9] Like a marriage vow, a proposal of marriage goes better with a first name—the right first name—as Barbara Pym observes in *Crampton Hodnet* (New York, 1985), 91–92:

> His voice took on a more hopeful note. "Oh, Miss Morrow—Janie," he burst out suddenly.
>
> "My name isn't Janie."
>
> "Well, it's something beginning with J," he said impatiently. It was annoying to be held up by such a triviality. What did it matter what her name was at this moment?

"Swans in the air. Swans in the air. / Let the chosen one appear." And the Curate reads the piece of paper: "Alan Norman." Like Karl Marx, Alan materializes out of nowhere to save a society passive in its expectations, wanting a fairy-tale happy ending to fulfill its hopes.

The stanzas which functioned as virtually a prayer for redemption in the 1931 poem ("Let this be kept as a generous hour by all") appear in *Dogskin* during Alan's quest for Sir Francis as a mockery of hyperbolic romantic expectations. They are preceded by Alan's preposterous statements about what he would do to have the "shopwindow dummy" he has met on his trip come alive and be a faithful lover:

> I would hunt the enormous whale in the Arctic lowlands,
> I would count all the starlings in the British Islands,
> I would run through fighting Europe in absolute silence.
>
> (*DBS* 142)

After such utterances, "The landlocked state shall get its port today" sounds like a lover's delusion, and not a visitation of grace. Only in fantasy does erotic love redeem the world.

The last scene's revelation that Iris, during Alan's absence, has become engaged to a "munitions manufacturer" is thus only the last of many signs that engagements and marriage vows may be empty rituals. One rejected version of the last scene dramatizes with particular irony the predominance of aesthetic form over spiritual significance. In this draft, a resisting Iris, still faithful to Alan, is forced to marry her new fiancé. According to the stage directions, "Fireworks go off. Balloons rise. Bells toll" to celebrate the marriage, and a chorus of villagers sings a wedding madrigal (by way of *The Tempest* and "Alexander's Feast"):

> O day of joy in happiness abounding
> Streams through the hills with laughter are resounding
> For Pressan is delighted
> To see you thus united
> Handsome he
> Lovely she

Riches, children, every blessing
Be to you for your possessing
Love be round you everywhere
Happy Happy Happy Pair.[10]

Happiness certainly does not abound in the bride, who is in tears during all the festivities. The occasion has everything but love and joy. The grand finale satisfies the deepest aesthetic needs of the villagers. Singing in chorus—like the Mendelssohn chorus at the end of *The Dance of Death*—they participate in the ritual. The bride and groom are virtually unnecessary, exploited for theatrical requirements. "Iris is born [sic] to church," say Auden's handwritten stage directions, implying the requisitioning of a young woman for a dramatic role.

Although *Dogskin* implicitly denies the power of marriage to "save," its epilogue nevertheless affirms a "charity" whose source it does not specify: "Choose therefore that you may recover; both your charity and your place." By 1938, in his review of Laurence Housman's biography of A. E. Housman, Auden had separated "marriage" entirely from charity:

> Heaven and Hell. Reason and Instinct. Conscious Mind and Unconscious. . . . Yes, the two worlds. Perhaps the Socialist State will marry them; perhaps the only thing which can bring them together is the experience of what Christians call Charity.[11]

In 1931 Auden had imagined, in mock apocalyptic excitement, "The two worlds in each other's arms." Toward the end of the decade, "marriage" was not enough to inspire such an embrace. It took—Auden used the word with an explicitly religious qualification—"what Christians call Charity."

In its brief allusion to a fragment of a wedding, *On the Frontier* offers a feeble echo of *Paid on Both Sides* and *The Dance of Death*. As Anna Vrodny and Eric Thorwald, the

[10] From a prompt copy of *The Dog beneath the Skin* in the Group Theatre Archive, Henry W. and Albert A. Berg Collection of the New York Public Library, Astor, Lenox, and Tilden Foundations.

[11] Auden, "Jehovah Housman and Satan Housman," *New Verse* 28 (January 1938): 16–17.

star-crossed lovers of Ostnia and Westland, meet at the symbolic space which is the border between their warring countries, Anna's drunken Uncle Oswald "is humming the Wedding March from *Lohengrin*." He has no conscious knowledge that Eric will a moment later call "despairingly" across the frontier to Anna. The humming is Auden's rather heavy-handed indication of what is not to be. In this play both bride and bridegroom die, pathetic victims whose love is crushed by the war between their countries. Unlike the love of Nower and Shaw, this one was unknown to both societies, and no one ever vested any hope in its redemptive powers. Like the Mendelssohn march, the music from *Lohengrin* evokes those "bridal pairs" Auden could not write into the resolution.

III

Only one year after *On the Frontier* Auden composed the grand finale he had been trying to complete since *Paid on Both Sides*. The unfulfilled epithalamion of 1928—

> With gift in hand we come
> From every neighbour farm
> To celebrate in wine
> The certain union of
> A woman and a man
>
> (*CLP* 32)

—was fulfilled in the epithalamion of 1939:

> . . . this quiet wedding of
> A Borgese and a Mann
> Planted human unity.
>
> (*AT* 107)

Giuseppe Antonio Borgese and Elizabeth Mann, whose different nationalities were perfectly suited to Auden's turn of mind and metaphor, could accomplish what John Nower and Anne Shaw, and Eric Thorwald and Anna Vrodny, could not: "Hostile kingdoms of the truth, / Fighting fragments of content, /

Here were reconciled by love." And unlike the epithalamion for Alan Sinkinson and Iris Snodgrass, this one, appearing at the end of the volume *Another Time*, could by its position provide a comic ending and a ritual of incorporation for all the isolated people (Housman, Arnold, Melville) in the book's earlier poems.

Auden makes grand claims for this couple: their powers encompass great stretches of space and time, all of Europe and several hundred years of history. In one of his favorite topoi, Auden traces the intellectual and cultural fragmentation of the present back to the Renaissance.[12] The Middle Ages are considered a time of social and cultural unity:

> A priori dogmas brought
> Into one collective will
> All of European thought.
>
> (*AT* 107)

But the economic and social dislocations of the early Renaissance "broke eternity in two." The mythic medieval past resembles the buried origin of the feud between the Nowers and Shaws, and justifies the need for a marriage in the present time.

Auden burdens the names "Giuseppe Borgese" and "Elizabeth Mann," as earlier he had burdened the names "Alan" and "Iris," with a monumental redemptive task. Allusions throughout the poem to Dante, Leonardo, Shakespeare, and Quakers, in chronological order, give the epithalamion a cultural scope also, so that the final stanza's cast of characters seems to stand in for all the people in the poem and in the volume alike. Here creators of Western culture (a select group of Auden's favorites) from the eighteenth century onward are apotheosized into an order of deities offering benediction to the assembled guests:

> Vowing to redeem the State,
> Now let every girl and boy

[12] For a fuller discussion of this topos of Auden's invention, see "The Myth of the Seventeenth Century" in McDiarmid, *Saving Civilization*.

To the heaven of the great
All their prayers and praises lift;
Mozart with ironic breath
Turning poverty to song,
Goethe ignorant of sin
Placing every human wrong,
Blake the industrious visionary,
Tolstoi the great animal,
Hellas-loving Hölderlin,
Wagner who obeyed his gift
Organized his wish for death
Into a tremendous cry,
Looking down upon us, all
        Wish us joy.

(*AT* 110)

Auden pulls out all the stops and lets loose with the kind of fanfare he rejected for *Dogskin*. The choir that suddenly materializes, directed by Presenter Auden ("Now let . . ."), resembles the chorus of villagers singing the organist's "Happy Happy Happy" madrigal. But this is more than incidental music, because these boys and girls are "Vowing to redeem the State." The singing children and the artistic deities alike resemble the bridal pairs in their ring dance, whose harmonious movements signified warmth and pardon. With their different nationalities and idiosyncrasies ("Turning poverty to song," "ignorant of sin," "industrious visionary"), the deities also form a harmony of distinct and peculiar individuals. Unified in the act of blessing, they form a further model of reconciliation.

The actors in this showy, theatrical, resounding resolution take some of the ceremonial burden off the bride and groom, whose resonant names are really all that Auden needs ("Borgese" and "Mann" cast almost as much of a nimbus as "Goethe" and "Blake"). Rather carefully, in fact, the poem limits the powers attributed to the couple. Their "bed of marriage" is only a "symbol now of the rebirth / Asked of old humanity." The closest Auden comes to making any connection between their love and international peace is the first stanza's metaphor about the seed's becoming the tree. If, some miraculous day, "human unity" comes into being, "savants may" trace its origin to this wedding. The mood is conditional, and phrases like "kingdoms of the truth" and "modern policy" refer only to the microcosm.

Throughout the epithalamion Auden stops short of implying that weddings cause anything like a "generous hour" of universal forgiveness. At best, the Mann-Borgese nuptial provides the occasion for a lot of cultural name-dropping and energetic public language. For Auden it inspires yet one more vision of an ideal, unified Europe, like that of the scholars who "see Superstition overcome / As all national frontiers melt / In a true imperium," or of Dante,

> When, a total failure in
> An inferior city, he
> Dreaming out his anger, saw
> All the scattered leaves of fact
> Bound by love
>
> (*AT* 108)

or of Leonardo, who

> Jostled by the sights of war
> And unpleasant greedy men,
> At Urbino watched a dove. . . .
>
> (*AT* 109)

The connection between any of these visions and an actual "imperium" of European nations exists only in the realm of wish.

In addition, unlike the Alan Sinkinson and Iris Snodgrass of Auden's poem, these lovers have a certain psychological complexity. As he moved toward the bedroom in the 1931 epithalamion Auden talked about sex as a cure for cancer and headaches. Here, anticipating *The Sea and the Mirror*, Auden uses characters from *The Tempest* to advise the lovers on deeper matters:

Shame at our shortcomings makes
Lame magicians of us all,
Forcing our invention to
An illegal miracle
And a theatre of disguise;
Brilliantly your angels took
Every lover's role for you,
Wore seduction like a mask
Or were frigid for your sakes;
Set these shadows, now your eyes
On the whole of substance look,
Free to-day.

(*AT* 109)

However confident and assertive the trochaic meter makes the lines sound, they imply that human love, even between a Borgese and a Mann, is not always perfectly reconciled. Feelings of inadequacy may make lovers escape into fantasies; that "illegal miracle" is what Auden was later to call (in "Compline") "vain fornications of fancy." Now that the lovers are married—now that their eyes look on "the whole of substance," the love of an actual person—they need no longer indulge in the fantasies formerly supplied by their "angels," who become sexually aggressive or frigid according to desire. And in the following stanza, Auden suggests that the lovers will have to forgive each other's faults ("Every timid vice forgive"). They are a long way from Iris and Alan, whose marriage inspired forgiveness in others. Here almost parenthetically Auden begins to differentiate between a "wedding" and a "marriage," where real forgiveness is a requirement, not an incidental effect.

The stanza-form demands that each topic be resolved in three syllables, and the resounding chords of the final stanza overwhelm any earlier dissonance. And the entire poem, placed at the end of *Another Time*, performs a similar function for the preceding poems of the volume, resonantly concluding them all on a note of artificial gaiety. This epithalamion is, after all, a poem Auden chose not to reprint after 1945.

The volume's overall structure is that of a Shakespearean comedy: in the separate lyric poems of the first section ("People and Places") the characters express sadness and frustration privately, and in the final section ("Occasional Poems") they join together in a public ritual to reconstitute a society. To use Auden's own terms, the sad, peculiar, eccentric separate beings in the lyrics are like the thief, the nephew, and the asthmatic clerk of the 1931 epithalamion, people whose lonely isolation is redeemed in a grand nuptial ceremony.

The epigraph of *Another Time* anticipates this structure, both the isolation and the community:

> Every eye must weep alone
> Till I Will be overthrown.
>
> But I Will can be removed,
> Not having sense enough
> To guard against I Know,
> But I Will can be removed.
>
> Then all I's can meet and grow,
> I Am become I Love,
> I Have Not I Am Loved,
> Than all I's can meet and grow.
>
> Till I Will be overthrown
> Every eye must weep alone.
>
> (*AT* vii)

In the last poem of the volume all "I's" do "meet," artificially, as the implied guests of the wedding, as the boys and girls of the choir, and as the idiosyncratic artists who bless "us all." The community so aggressively asserted evolves from separate "I's," most of them weeping.

The epigraph focuses on the barrier between the lonely self and other people; between "I Will" (what I want, what I insist on, what I determine) and "I Love." Until the egotism of "I

Will" is "overthrown," the eye or I must weep alone. Once that change occurs, the self's boundaries dissolve in charity, and "I Am becomes I Love." Or, as Auden says in another poem in the volume, with I/eye in mind, "there is no such thing as a vain look." The epigraph does not distinguish between the romantic feelings of two lovers and the general social love that underlies communities. Both find their origin in agape, neighborly love, and both depend on removing "I Will."

The epigraph's pun links the "I" of selfishness with the weeping "eye," and associates love with the plural "all I's." Its repeated opening and closing line is ambiguous. It seems to imply that the condition of isolated misery will continue until "I Will be overthrown," but the emphasis can also be placed on the word "alone." The point may not be that the self stops weeping when it is loved, but that it no longer need weep *alone.* (In "The Shield of Achilles," charity is a condition in which "one could weep because another wept.")

Throughout the volume, people weep in isolation. Housman, repressing his sorrow, "Kept tears like dirty postcards in a drawer." In "Dover," the "eyes of the returning" may be "filled with the tears of the beaten." Dover is a place where "Each one prays in the dusk for himself." Eros Paidagogos, considering the unfulfilled loves of Oxford, "Weeps on his virginal bed," and "over the talkative city like any other / Weep the non-attached angels." But the expression of feeling may signal a change: as the speaker of "Schoolchildren" asks, "The storm of tears shed in the corner, are these / The seeds of the new life?" For Edward Lear, they are; he "wept to himself in the night," but "guided by tears he successfully reached his Regret." In "As I walked out one evening" the release of tears signals the end of a narcissistic love that is both dry and frozen:

> "O stand, stand at the window
>   As the tears scald and start;
> You shall love your crooked neighbour
>   With your crooked heart."
>
> (*AT* 43)

In part 2, the more ironic but not particularly humorous "Lighter Poems," the characters exist in unredeemed isolation. James Honeyman, whose poison gas will choke the world, "didn't laugh or cry" as a child. Victor's "tears came tumbling down," yet he soon stabs his wife to death. And of the paradigmatic tyrant Auden writes (in "Epitaph on a Tyrant"), "And when he cried the little children died in the streets." His tears, like Victor's, lead to massacre.

In the "Occasional Poems" all private miseries are put in a larger social context, and, in the rather artificial manner of the public poems, tears are redeemed. These poems cover all the forms of "saving" that interested Auden in the 1930s: political ("Spain 1937"), literary ("In Memory of W. B. Yeats"), psychological ("In Memory of Sigmund Freud"), nuptial (the epithalamion). The furtive tears of frustrated eros become the compassionate tears of agape; every "I" does not weep alone. In "Spain 1937" all "I's" meet and grow in the community formed by social action: "They came to present their lives." The "shared cigarette" and the "Fumbled and unsatisfactory embrace before hurting" are instances, however doomed, of overthrowing "I Will." The role of the poet (in "In Memory of W. B. Yeats") is to release the sympathy latent in every "I": "And the seas of pity lie / Locked and frozen in each eye." And Freud heals, internally and psychologically, the divisions that the bride and groom of the final poem will join in their marriage, those "unequal moieties fractured / By our own well-meaning sense of justice."

The elegies for Yeats and Freud must precede the epithalamion: not only because the whole volume looks forward from its first poem to the "defeat of grief," and rejoicing follows mourning, but because the sympathy released by the poet and the internal reconciliation wrought by psychoanalysis must precede marriage. Freud's death creates a community of mourners, eyes weeping together:

> . . . over a grave
> The household of Impulse mourns one dearly loved.

Sad is Eros, builder of cities,
And weeping anarchic Aphrodite.

(*AT* 106)

The final weepers of the volume are the earlier ones transformed. The Eros who wept in frustration in "Oxford" now grieves over "one dearly loved"; the impulses previously thwarted or directed narcissistically to the self are now directed outward in charitable love. So transformed, erotic drives will in the final poem be ritually sanctioned and blessed in a public ceremony.

But in a way these tears are like Iris's in the *Dogskin* manuscript, expressions of feeling overwhelmed by hoopla and fanfare and silly ceremonies. Auden had finally written the grand finale he wanted, but it was necessarily bombastic and "woozy." By the time *Another Time* appeared in February 1940, Auden had outgrown the simple spiritual intensities of the occasional poems. Their ambiguous language already suggested a weakened faith. (In subsequent years all were radically altered or withheld from publication.) Soon—quite soon—Auden was writing about marriage rather than weddings, and in a way suggested by the stanzas of the 1939 epithalamion directed to the lovers' private life, advising them to abandon fantasies and to forgive one another.

The Form of Solemnization of Matrimony in *The Book of Common Prayer* is alluded to in the title "In Sickness and in Health" (autumn 1940), but the title, like the poem itself, emphasizes the faultiness of married love:

Dear, all benevolence of fingering lips
That does not ask forgiveness is a noise
    At drunken feasts. . . .

(*AT* 29)

The wedding poems and plays of the early thirties built up to the marriage ceremony, with its guests, its vows, its musical fanfares, its festivities. "In Sickness and in Health" focuses exclusively on life after the great public ritual moment, praying with some desperation of tone "That this round O of faithfulness we swear / May never wither to an empty nought." Unlikely to save any society or inspire warmth and pardon, these lovers (Auden himself and Chester Kallman) depend on another source of grace:

> Rejoice, dear love, in Love's peremptory word;
> All chance, all love, all logic, you and I,
> Exist by grace of the Absurd. . . .
>
> (*CP* 32)

By 1940 Auden's idea of married love had become dissociated from its ceremonial origin and secularized. He no longer depended on lovers to hallow and reanimate society. The symbols of wedded love had now some personal significance—Auden had bought Kallman and himself gold rings and had sent his brother a postcard from them both with the message "Honeymoon Greetings"—but so also had its disillusions.[13] In a manuscript notebook from 1941–1942 Auden uses marriage as a metaphor in a new way:

> In spite of obvious differences, it is not altogether misleading
> To describe the relationship of oneself to one's vocational gift
> By the analogy of a marriage. It is much more difficult
> Than we ever imagined when we took our vows
> And it rarely turns out to be happy.[14]

In these poems from the early 1940s the way that spiritual value exists "outside" the work of art begins to change: it no longer exists on the same plane as the rest of the story, a fifth act excised, festivities cut short or thwarted. Now anything of worth to the spirit, forgiveness, reconciliation, love, exists in extraceremonial life. In *The Magic Flute*, said Auden in a 1943 speech, "the trials are over in the twinkling of an eye, whereas in life, not only do they last forever, but also they are not antecedent to, but coterminous with marriage."[15] In the work of

[13] Auden's postcard to his brother is in the Berg Collection, New York Public Library.

[14] Holograph notebook in the Berg Collection, New York Public Library.

[15] From an unpublished speech in the Auden Collection, McCabe Library, Swarthmore College.

art, the opera, the Shakespearean comedy, the wedding ceremony—in all of these reconciliation and charity appear automatic, instantaneous, absolute, *whereas in life* they are more difficult to discover. The generous hour inspired by the magic ceremonial moment has become the lifetime "from this day forward," when powers beyond those of bride and groom, Mozart and Mendelssohn, are needed.

CHAPTER THREE

The Other Side of the Mirror: *New Year Letter*, *For the Time Being*, and *The Sea and the Mirror*

A great while ago the world begun,
  Hey, ho, the wind and the rain,
But that's all one, our play is done,
  And we'll strive to please you every day.
—Shakespeare, *Twelfth Night*

"WHEREAS IN LIFE": this unobtrusive phrase from Auden's 1943 speech lies at the heart of the long poems Auden was writing in the early 1940s. Whereas in life: the phrase implies two planes, one artificial, one not. Whereas-in-life is built into the genres of *New Year Letter* (written 1940), *For the Time Being* (written 1941–1942), and *The Sea and the Mirror* (written 1942–1944), genres otherwise unalike: a letter substitutes for the voice, the performers of an oratorio look out at the life they mimic, the "commentary" on *The Tempest* situates itself after the play. The long poems adopt the stance of the *plaudite*: acknowledging their own artifice, they look out at the audience and recognize the separation between that world and their own.

In the classical *plaudite*, cheerful, energetic, concise, the actors request the satisfaction of knowing that they are professionally successful. (The dramatists did, after all, compete for prizes at the Athenian dramatic festivals.) At the end of Menander's *Dyskolos*, in one of the earliest surviving *plaudites*, the slave Getas addresses the audience directly as "youths, boys, men," and treats the performance of the play as a kind of feat to be appreciated, like an athletic exploit:

Well, if you've all enjoyed our victory
With this old nuisance, we request your kind
Applause—youths, boys and men! May Victory,
That merry virgin, born of noble line,
Attend us with her favour all our days![1]

At the end of Terence's *Andria* the slave Davos turns the spatial distinction between inside, in the "house," and outside, on the street, into an ontological distinction between the characters' world and the audience's (like Armado's "You that way: we this way" at the end of *Love's Labor's Lost*):

DAVOS. You needn't wait till they come out again: the betrothal will take place indoors and any other business that remains.
CANTOR. Clap your hands.[2]

Shakespeare's *plaudites* introduce into the tradition more explicit awareness of levels of reality; they concede to the audience with a flourish. The deference is that of servant to master, entertainer to audience, art to life. It is part of the actor's role, as artificial as plumes and tights and wigs: "If we shadows have offended"; "We'll strive to please you every day"; "or else my project fails, / Which was to please. . . ."

The Shakespearean twist to the *plaudite* creates an attitude that is characteristic of Auden. In Auden's long poems of the early 1940s the deferential stance informs the whole work. No mere eight or ten lines at the end, the *plaudite* is what the poem reveals itself to be. In its genre, in its consciousness of its own artifice, in its ritualized act of concession to something ontologically and spiritually superior, each poem undermines its own authority and indicates through its obeisance a value outside itself. The contrast "whereas-in-life" informs these works: all are situated at borders between a work of art and a hypothetical audience, so that the notion of an audience to whom a *plaudite* would be addressed is already contained

[1] Menander, *Dyskolos*, ed. and trans. W. G. Arnott, in *Menander*, vol. 1 (Cambridge and London, 1979), 355.

[2] Terence, *Andria*, ed. and trans. John Sargeaunt, in *Terence*, vol. 1 (Cambridge and London, 1912, 1986), 109.

within the poem. The "letter" is addressed to Elizabeth Mayer, who is apostrophized in the text several times; the Narrator of *For the Time Being* speaks out to the oratorio's hypothetical audience, which may also be a diffuse group of readers; and *The Sea and the Mirror* includes a Stage Manager who addresses Critics, a Prompter, and a character whose monologue, "Caliban to the Audience," addresses the hypothetical audience of a hypothetical performance of *The Tempest*.[3]

The world "outside" that these hypothetical audiences inhabit acquires spiritual worth in a rather complex manner. The poems all include "wedding feasts" like the endings manqué of the 1930s plays, festive events associated with communal renewal, forgiveness, and an exalted state of mind. Mozart, Buxtehude, choral and operatic voices, and solemn musics fill the air. However, each of the three long poems rejects its wedding feast as trumpery, mere spectacle and special effects with no spiritual value. In so undermining its own production, the poem invokes the world of its hypothetical audiences and locates genuine forgiveness there.

Genuine or nonartificial: increasingly, the poems call attention not to the reality of spiritual significance somewhere else,

[3] As early as 1929 Auden was interested in the possibilities of the *plaudite*. Auden and Isherwood's little-known play *The Enemies of a Bishop* ends with Robert Bicknell's extended address to the audience. Although the passage does not ask for applause, it closely resembles the *plaudite* of classical drama because the character starts to leave the stage, then turns and addresses the audience. Bicknell's comments invoke the contrast between the world of the players and the world of the audience: "Remain we here / Sitting too late among the lights and music." However, instead of insisting on his own *un*reality, as Auden's speakers do in the forties, Bicknell claims a status as "real" as the audience's:

> If when the curtain falls, if you should speak,
> Turning together, as of neighbours lately gone,
> Although our anguish seem but summer lightning,
> Sudden, soon over, in another place,
> Although immune then, do not say of us
> "It was nothing, their loss." It was all.

See Auden and Isherwood, *Plays, and Other Dramatic Writings*, 78–79.

"whereas-in-life," but to their own *inability* to show or express forgiveness. The act of concession becomes the poem's own self-condemnation rather than an homage to some forgiving, spiritually worthy being "outside" the poem's own text or performance. In calling God "the smiling / Secret [he] cannot quote" and in identifying "silence" with "ripeness" and "ripeness" with "all," *The Sea and the Mirror* implies that there is no language for ultimate value. If it cannot be quoted, no poem could possibly "signify" it. If it is "silence," naming or describing it lies outside the capacities of language altogether. The poem may be only a guilty, tinselly performance incapable of any significance at all except to call attention to its own guilty, tinselly self. Elizabeth Mayer is morally and spiritually remote from *New Year Letter*'s speaker, but he does invoke her as "Forgiving, helping all we do" and refers to two visits to her house; even before she sees the opening lines of the poem the reader sees the dedication to Mayer. But who is the source of the "authentic molar pardon" in *The Sea and the Mirror*? Because the poem has already undermined its own ability to give a name to such a power, a reader would be hard pressed to state before whom Caliban performs his act of concession. No longer signifiable, "outside" the poem exists only as a rhetorical projection of its own literary character.

New Year Letter

Why a *letter* to Elizabeth Mayer? An exercise in the discursive Augustan verse-epistolary mode: this reasonable, easygoing explanation has satisfied most critics of Auden's poetry.[4] It allows for the rambling, chatty mode of the letter, links it vaguely with the 1936 *Letter to Lord Byron*, suggests without laboring Auden's nascent conservatism, prepares the groundwork for the later Horatian Auden, and by its looseness disarms disagreement. *New Year Letter* is chatty, topical, allusive, wide-ranging—all the epithets used of Pope's *Epistle to*

[4] See Callan, *Auden*, 172; Fuller, *Reader's Guide*, 132; Richard Johnson, *Man's Place: An Essay on Auden* (Ithaca, 1973), 5–8.

Burlington fit. Yet so is the *Letter to Lord Byron*, a very different poem indeed. And so is much of "later" Auden: his chattiness irritates those readers who prefer the earlier anxious, apocalyptic Auden.

In writing a letter Auden could exploit the genre's connotations of both "naturalness" and "literariness." Insofar as a letter is "natural," a "substitute for direct speech," it links two actual people; it "projects an image of its author at a given point in time and negotiates a relationship with a particular reader."[5] It exists as part of a nontextual world, of historical people with a friendship outside their epistolary relation, people whose names could be found in a telephone directory for 1940, or, as Auden says elsewhere, whose "existences and histories could be verified by a private detective" (*HC* 42). Thus the "friend Elizabeth" who is invoked exists truly (or did at the time of the letter's composition and of its original publication), a breathing, sentient being beyond the black and white of the printed poem.

Insofar as *New Year Letter* is a "literary" work, it adopts certain conventions of the verse epistle, not only its chattiness, but its awareness of a wider audience than Elizabeth Mayer. The letter is available "to all / Who wish to read it anywhere," and its prolix commentary on current events, European culture, romanticism, and American history bulks larger than it would be likely to in a merely personal letter. Auden's diplomatic metaphor allows the letter a public dimension and function, yet suggests that the "good offices of verse" are being used in a psychomachia, not a war:

> May such heart and intelligence
> As huddle now in conference

[5] Mireille Bossis, "Methodological Journeys through Correspondences," in *Men/Women of Letters*, *Yale French Studies* 71 (1986), ed. Charles A. Porter, 63; and Janet Gurkin Altman, "The Letter Book as a Literary Institution 1539–1789: Toward a Cultural History of Published Correspondences in France," in *Men/Women of Letters*, 18–19. For a verse epistle that comments on this subject itself, see Marilyn Hacker's "Feeling and Form" in *Taking Notice* (New York, 1980), 3–5.

Whenever an impasse occurs
Use the good offices of verse. . . .

(*CP* 274)

In spite of its "good offices," *New Year Letter* stands condemned as a locus of Auden's "crimes," which are predominately literary. The poem cannot exempt itself from the faults its speaker confesses: "Time and again have slubbered through / With slip and slapdash what I do, / Adopted what I would disown, / The preacher's loose immodest tone." The guilt is located in Auden and particularly in what he writes. "Outside" this guilty collocation of self and poem exist three distinct levels of spiritual goodness: the "Great masters" of literature, a "summary tribunal" invoked for self-judgment; beyond this panel of judging fathers, beyond literature altogether, the forgiving mother, Elizabeth Mayer; and beyond these quasi-parental figures, a God apostrophized at the end of *New Year Letter* in a series of Dantesque metaphors ("O Unicorn among the cedars . . . O Dove of science . . . O Ichthus . . . O sudden Wind . . . O Clock and Keeper of the years").

Some background on the "summary tribunal": the abasement before other, spiritually superior literary figures occurs so often in Auden's poetry that it constitutes a topos; perhaps one could call it the *veneratio poetarum* (veneration of the poets).[6] Such a *veneratio* occurs in "At the Grave of Henry James" (1941), where James is addressed as "Master of nuance and scruple" and asked to pray for Auden. James himself is invoked for the spiritual standards that he maintained as an artist:

. . . your heart, fastidious as
A delicate nun, remained true to the rare noblesse
Of your lucid gift. . . .

(*CP* 129)

[6] For the suggestion of the word *veneratio* I am grateful to Professor John Hunt of the Classics Department of Villanova University.

"Yours be the disciplinary image that holds / Me back from agreeable wrong," Auden apostrophizes, and concludes by undermining his own spiritual worth:

> Pray for me and for all writers living or dead;
> Because there are many whose works
> Are in better taste than their lives; because there is no end
> To the vanity of our calling. . . .
>
> (*CP* 130)

In the late poem "The Cave of Making" Auden invokes the shade of Louis MacNeice to "break the spell of our self-enchantment," and apologizes for his "egocentric monologue." In the posthumously published "A Thanksgiving," Auden addresses Hardy, Thomas, Frost, Goethe, and others, and comments self-deprecatingly, "without You I couldn't have managed / Even my weakest of lines."

The panel of judging poets invoked in the first part of *New Year Letter* is addressed collectively as "Great Masters." They are praised, as Henry James is in the poem Auden wrote a year later, for their spiritual discipline—

> All the more honor to you then
> If, weaker than some other men,
> You had the courage that survives
> Soiled, shabby, egotistic lives
>
> (*CP* 268)

—and they have some of his religious remoteness: "Now large, magnificent, and calm, / Your changeless presences disarm / The sullen generations." Imagining them as a tribunal, Auden judges himself as spiritually lacking, "afraid / That he's unworthy of his trade," and desperately eager for approval: "O who can show convincing proof / That he is worthy of their love?" A "weak offender," he "must / Beg for leniency."

Dante, Blake, and Rimbaud, the chief of these judges, are chosen because of the way they perceived values beyond those of literature. At some decisive moment each chose a larger, more comprehensive vision of the universe. Dante "spoiled a temporal career / And to the supernatural brought / His passion." In the *Paradiso* he described a "juster nucleus than Rome / Where love had its creative home." Blake "heard inside each mortal thing / Its holy emanation sing." And the "young Rimbaud," "Skilful, intolerant and quick, / . . . strangled an old rhetoric." Blake, envisioning a holy, animate universe, and Rimbaud, abandoning poetry when he had no more to say, concede literature's secondary importance. These stern visionaries offer models of self-discipline, especially for the self that slubbers and preaches.

Outside the world of male writers who remind Auden of his own imperfection, outside poetry altogether, dwells Elizabeth Mayer.[7] The sun shines and the music sounds whenever she enters the poem. In the poem's opening section she is introduced through the sun, which

> Lit up America and on
> A cottage on Long Island shone
> Where Buxtehude as we played
> One of his *passacaglias* made
> Our minds a *civitas* of sound
> Where nothing but assent was found. . . .
>
> (*CP* 266)

From light, to music, to heavenly order, Elizabeth Mayer grows in power as Auden moves from one level of allusion to another. Later in the poem Auden begins another passage describing a visit to her with the phrase, "Warm in your house, Elizabeth," adding a cozy maternal warmth to the sunlight from the earlier passage.

At the very end "Dear friend Elizabeth," merging with the sun that lit up her cottage and the warmth of her house, becomes, herself, the sun:

[7] Stan Smith remarks that *New Year Letter* is "dedicated to a mother-figure" and is "in one sense a confession of phallic incompetence in a world at war, dominated by the penis rivalries of a patriarchal order." See *W. H. Auden* (Oxford and New York, 1985), 153.

Who on the lives about you throw
A calm *solificatio*,
A warmth throughout the universe. . . .

(*CP* 316)

(Calmness is a quality Elizabeth Mayer shares with Dante, Blake, and Rimbaud in the idealized versions of them Auden presents. For a poet whose life was characterized by anxiety, calmness was an important attribute of deities.) In the last line of the *Paradiso* it is "Love that moves the Sun and the other stars." Auden rearranges the images when he says that "love illuminates again," and the wording associates Elizabeth Mayer and her "*solificatio*" with divine love. Spreading a "warmth throughout the universe," she is obviously *outside* its guilt and anxiety.

The second of *New Year Letter*'s two codas is addressed to Elizabeth Mayer: in Auden's poem, Beatrice outranks God. God, like another but more vaguely conceived great poetic master, is asked in the penultimate prayer to be a disciplinarian:

Disturb our negligence and chill,
Convict our pride of its offence
In all things, even penitence. . . .

(*CP* 315)

Somewhat more positively than the earlier judges, God will "Send strength sufficient for our day, / And point our knowledge on its way." From a traditional, theological perspective, God is the most "outside" of the various ranks of deities called on in *New Year Letter*. But the poem saves its final act of concession, its ultimate apostrophe, for Elizabeth Mayer:

We fall down in the dance, we make
The old ridiculous mistake,
But always there are such as you
Forgiving, helping what we do.

(*CP* 316)

Invoking her in association with the sun, and then invoking the love that "illuminates" the world, Auden's poem ends looking out over a border that is psychological, spiritual, ontological.

Elizabeth Mayer is also the deity who presides over weddings. The Christmas dinner that Auden had, in actual historical fact, eaten at her house the week before, metamorphoses in *New Year Letter* into the kind of nuptial occasion always just beyond the powers of the characters in the 1930s plays.[8] Insofar as *New Year Letter* is a kind of *Divine Comedy* manqué, this passage, at the opening of the third section, parallels the vision of Beatrice in Paradise in the opening canto of the *Paradiso*. At this visit, an "unexpected power" transformed the meal into a sacred event:

> Warm in your house, Elizabeth
> A week ago at the same hour
> I felt the unexpected power
> That drove our ragged egos in
> From the dead-ends of greed and sin
> To sit down at the wedding feast,
> Put shining garments on the least,
> Arranged us so that each and all,
> The erotic and the logical,
> Each felt the *placement* to be such
> That he was honored overmuch,
> And SCHUBERT sang and MOZART played
> And GLUCK and food and friendship made
> Our privileged community. . . .
>
> (*CP* 290)

The nuptial language and the musical trappings of the thirties are present in *New Year Letter*'s wedding feast, but the emphasis is on a general feeling of reconciliation. This is the inverse of the wedding celebration in the *Dogskin* manuscript, where a tearful Iris is dragged to her wedding by General and Mrs. Hotham, and the pressure of society's aesthetic and emo-

[8] See Carpenter, *W. H. Auden*, 286.

tional needs requires the ceremony. Here no one is "married," yet everyone present becomes part of a loving community of souls. All the separate "ragged egos," erotic, logical, divided by idiosyncrasies, are driven in toward each other from the "dead-ends of greed and sin." The centripetal power of love draws them together, counteracting the centrifugal selfish forces.

As if to emphasize a divine presence blessing the wedding feast, Auden blends two weddings from biblical parables: the one in Matthew 22:2–14, about the king who sees a man without a wedding garment at his son's wedding feast and orders the man "cast . . . into outer darkness"; and the wedding described in Luke 14:8–11, where Christ advises the Pharisees not to sit in the "highest room" at a wedding, lest the host want to save the seat for someone more important and say, "Give this man place." It is better, says Christ, to sit in the "lowest room," so the host may invite you to move higher, and "then shalt thou have worship in the presence of them that sit at meat with thee." The dinner at Elizabeth Mayer's combines the best of both parables: the power of divine love has put wedding garments on everyone, and the guests' "placement" is such that everyone has "worship" in the presence of the others at the meal.

Manuscript revisions of this passage make it clear that Auden did not originally conceive of the Christmas dinner he had enjoyed the week before as a wedding feast.[9] In the earliest extant version of the passage, the dinner was a merely musical occasion with no particular intensity. A rather iconographic "Christmas dove / Of faith and happiness and Love" descended on an amorphous "little company" at dinner. This dove was probably inspired by Charles Williams's *Descent of the Dove*, a book that Auden admired and that had just been published in 1939, and it is reminiscent of other doves and similarly communal occasions in Auden's poetry: the dove Leonardo looks at in the 1939 epithalamion, and the "dove-like

[9] For transcripts of the relevant parts of the manuscripts, see the appendix to this book.

powers" of the light in "A Summer Night" (*CP* 96). But it seems merely decorative in the original passage, though it already linked the occasion with ones of greater spiritual intensity. Unlike the dove, the "unexpected power" seems both external and internal, a power from outside the self that operates within and determines the ability to love.

The second manuscript is crucial in revealing the transition from the vague "little company" to the newly communal "each and all."[10] The text of the draft reveals Auden's uncertainty about singular and plural. In the marginal additions, "I" is scrawled over "We" (to define exactly who felt the unexpected power). Auden changed "each ragged ego" to "our ragged egos," joining the "I" of the passage with the group. The "dead-ends" of sin are first "his" (to go with "each"), then "our," then "the"—as if they existed independently of any individual sin.

The changes from "These evenings of last week-end" to "A week ago, Elizabeth" to "Warm in your house, Elizabeth," show Elizabeth Mayer increasing in power, as the proper name and the strongly placed adjective "warm" associate her benign, loving, maternal presence with the reconciliation Auden is about to describe. Her house becomes both womb and theater. The allusions to Matthew and Luke, particularly the phrase "shining garments" and the metaphor of the wedding feast, make the dinner both more spiritually exalted and more theatrical; they occur all in one sentence in a passage that Auden seems to have written in a flow with no subsequent changes. The "unexpected power," besides casting a religious aura over the guests, stage manages and directs. It drives the egos to sit down at the feast; it puts "shining garments" on the guests and it arranges them. When, after that arranging and the emotional change that results from it ("he was honored overmuch"), Auden writes, "And SCHUBERT sang and MOZART played," Schubert and Mozart seem to be singing and playing spontaneously and voluntarily, as the finishing touch of the "power." The emotionally charged quality of the pas-

[10] See appendix.

sage derives specifically from Auden's revisions in the manuscript. These changes show how forgiveness and love come into being in a give-and-take of unique, eccentric personalities, and in an atmosphere of special effects.

But this passage does not conclude the poem. Although *New Year Letter*'s wedding feast has the characteristics of the 1930s endings manqué, it is not a grand finale. As Auden wrote in that 1940 notebook, marriage "is much more difficult / than we ever imagined when we took our vows." The wedding feast is brief, the marriage long, and lovers do not always live in a generous hour of shining garments and Mozart. The very exaltation Auden added in the manuscript sets the whole experience on a different plane, from which the poem distances itself at the end.

There, the exalted metaphor of the wedding feast is changed into something more homely. Auden does not undermine the validity of the wedding feast; he undermines its permanence. Under Elizabeth Mayer's sympathetic influence, he has discovered the "truth / That no one marries," and

> That each for better or for worse
> Must carry round with him through life,
> A judge, a landscape, and a wife.
>
> (*CP* 316)

That "no one marries" suggests that the wedding feast does not have a permanently binding effect: it only shows what perfect reconciliation feels like. And yet "for better or for worse," writes Auden, echoing the Solemnization of Matrimony, we each "carry round with" us—like a burden—a "wife," a person to whom we have made a vow. The vow says that there is an interest more important to us than our own, and that we have a commitment to treat that person with neighborly love even when the wedding feast is over. The pardon of festival moments is not absolute.

By echoing the service from the *Book of Common Prayer* at the end of *New Year Letter*, particularly the part that describes the time in which the vows are operative, Auden opens out the poem at the end to all the postceremonial time ahead.

The poem ends at a margin, the border between "wedding" and "marriage." Elizabeth Mayer, invoked at the beginning of the coda, exists "outside" in many ways: she has a verifiable extratextual existence; she is associated with Auden's knowledge of the time "for better or for worse"; she is metaphorically "outside" ordinary people's lives, casting a warmth "throughout the universe"; and she is spiritually beyond Auden, who hopes that he may someday be "more worthy of your sympathy." As the person the poem is officially dedicated to, as well as the person called on within the poem, she is unquestionably beyond the paper words Auden has slubbered through (though the manuscript revisions show that the composition was not all slip and slapdash).

New Year Letter's final lines constitute a domestication of the spiritual effects of the wedding feast, a translation of the "unexpected power" into a daily loving of one's neighbor, as the young man who has traveled so far makes a New Year's vow to be more worthy:

O every day in sleep and labour
Our life and death are with our neighbour,
And love illuminates again
The city and the lion's den,
The world's great rage, the travel of young men.

(*CP* 316)

For the Time Being

The "erotic and the logical" reappear in *For the Time Being*, Auden's "Christmas Oratorio," as the shepherds and Wise Men, and again form a group united in neighborly love. This union also is essentially a reconciliation: it comes into being because "ragged egos" are driven into the center, individual selfish needs subordinated for the sake of all. In "At the Manger," in the center of the poem, Auden dramatizes operatically the fragmentedness, and finally the union, of the figures who meet at the Nativity. First the individual Wise Men sing separately, in "The Summons," and then together; then the three shepherds sing separately, and together; then they alternate as trios, and finally sing as "tutti":

TUTTI
We bless
WISE MEN
Our lives' impatience
SHEPHERDS
Our lives' laziness,
TUTTI
And bless each other's sin, exchanging here
WISE MEN
Exceptional conceit
SHEPHERDS
with average fear.
TUTTI
Released by love from isolating wrong
Let us for love unite our various song,
Each with his gift, according to his kind
Bringing this child his body and his mind.[11]

(*CP* 444–45)

As in *New Year Letter*'s wedding feast, opposed but complementary personalities form, temporarily, a community under the auspices of a benign maternal presence: there Elizabeth Mayer, here the Virgin Mary, whose song begins the section. The social harmony is reflected in the music: there Schubert's and Mozart's music, and Gluck's singing; here the operatic form. As the attribution of parts suggests, there is a blending and harmonizing, and not a cancelling out, of difference. In the shepherds and the Wise Men the chorus of boys and girls from the 1939 epithalamion reappears, as do the singing villagers of *Dogskin*'s unpublished ending.

New Year Letter's wedding feast occurred "a week ago" in a "cottage" on Long Island, in the house of the person to whom the poem is dedicated. *For the Time Being*'s wedding

[11] I have borrowed here from my analysis of this scene in "The Treason of the Clerks," in *Saving Civilization*, 105–6.

feast is more obviously theatrical: not a memory of a recent event, it exists as lines given to dramatic characters, the biblical figures of the Nativity. The poetic form—different for the different sets of characters, and for "tutti"—is more complex and artful, and the whole scene more "arranged." It embodies, formally, the idea of reconciliation, giving each character-type his own metric formula, and using a different one altogether for the utterances of the two sets when they are merged.

But this wedding feast, also, is no grand finale: it sits plumb in the middle of *For the Time Being*. In a subtle but unmistakable way the oratorio's structure undermines the spiritual worth of the scene: first presenting "At the Manger" as if it revealed ultimate value, the poem in its final section pulls the rug out from under itself and dismisses all its previous scenes as failed attempts at love.

To understand how the poem accomplishes such a reversal, *For the Time Being* must be seen in its overall framework. To a certain extent it looks like *New Year Letter*: a musical reconciliation in the center of the poem is surrounded by more ordinary life, less harmonious, less intense, less reconciled. *For the Time Being*'s legendary characters appear gradually, come together to create a pageant-like crèche in the poem's center, and gradually disappear, to be followed by the colloquial narrator who introduced the poem. Secular characters are gradually replaced by sacred ones. Then, after the reconciliation of "At the Manger," the sacred characters disappear, to be replaced by secular ones again.

The opening chorus expresses an apathy and despair that, like those of "The Burial of the Dead" in *The Waste Land*, are timeless. In spite of topical allusions to the "Portly Caesar" of the Roman Empire, the descent of "Darkness and snow" is necessarily recurrent: this is what it feels like to live only in the *saeculum*. The narrator's broad references to "this time of year" ally winter and December with the *saeculum* generally: its "physical pain and fiscal grief" are "familiar tribulations" in the Roman Empire, in 1941, and as long as there are people left to read *For the Time Being*. Allusions to generals, the navy, the "evil and armed," and the "political situation" link the year of Jesus Christ's birth with 1941, the year of the poem's composition (*CP* 409).

Like the presenter of a medieval drama, the narrator who speaks in our twentieth-century idiom ("living room," "juke box") and yet refers to an ancient Roman present ("the longest aqueduct in the world is under construction") mediates between a hypothetical contemporary audience and the Roman story. As he continues, the narrator gradually lets the generalized secular present recede, and introduces as setting the sacred world of the angel Gabriel, the Virgin Mary, Joseph, and all the other biblical figures from Matthew and Luke. In his dry, didactic way, he explains the ontological significance of the transition. Two references to mirrors frame the poem's sacred center: through the first of these, the narrator suggests that he must expose the insubstantiality of "our" world before he can reveal absolute reality.

> It's as if
> We had left our house for five minutes to mail a letter,
> And during that time the living room had changed places
> With the room behind the mirror over the fireplace;
> It's as if, waking up with a start, we discovered
> Ourselves stretched out flat on the floor, watching our
> shadow . . .
>
> (*CP* 410)

The ordinary, secular world is merely a mirror's reflection of some greater truth, insubstantial in spite of our conviction of its reality. With its evocation of Plato's parable of the cave, the simile announces a transvaluation of the notion of what is "real."

In the next few sections, the poem's characters will experience the same ontological shock. "The Annunciation," "The Temptation of St. Joseph," and "The Summons" introduce the familiar biblical characters, and in each case a messenger from a supernatural world—the angel Gabriel, the star of the Nativity, a chorus of angels—announces another reality. For those characters, as for us, the familiar construction of the world is philosophically challenged. In the center of the poem, "At the

Manger," the characters sing as if in the presence of ultimate spiritual truth.

In the final section ("The Flight into Egypt") the members of the Holy Family leave the sacred reality the poem has revealed and flee into the secular world of Egypt: "Mirror, let us through the glass / No authority can pass." The poem's setting exists now, presumably, back on the less real but more familiar side of the mirror, the one left behind after the poem's opening section. The narrator's final speech does in fact return us to the city and the "trying" time being, just as *New Year Letter*'s final lines returned to the "city and the lion's den."

But *For the Time Being* is not a symmetrical poem, sacred center tidily surrounded by secular edges, ultimate reality framed by the contingent, lesser reality that mirrors it. It is more complex: the narrator's final speech changes this expectation. With his nonchalant "Well, so that is that. Now we must dismantle the tree," the Narrator distances himself not only from the sacred center of the poem, but from all the previous sections of the poem:

> Now we must dismantle the tree,
> Putting the decorations back into their cardboard boxes—
> Some have got broken—and carrying them up to the attic.
> The holly and the mistletoe must be taken down and burnt. . . .
> (*CP* 465)

Talking exclusively as a twentieth-century person, the narrator pushes the Christmas story back into the Bible, along with the aqueducts and Caesar. The poem at the end tells you that it was only a poem: now it treats what you have seen not as absolute reality, a revelation of the sacred, but as a human creation that can be dismantled and stored in boxes. (Auden was so eager to create this distancing effect, it was so much the heart of this final speech, that—so the manuscript of the speech shows—he originally wrote as the first line "Take down the" and then crossed it out to begin with "Well.")[12] The Christmas story that the narrator refers to could not be

[12] Holograph manuscript in the Berg Collection, New York Public Library.

the ultimate reality mirrors reflect if it can be so artificially constructed and deconstructed.

In this speech the narrator separates the enactment of a rite from the original event it celebrates. The perfect harmony of "tutti" was merely a scene in a pageant, theology turned theater. What we remember, after Christmas, is not charity but failed human efforts,

> having drunk such a lot,
> Stayed up so late, attempted—quite unsuccessfully—
> To love all of our relatives, and in general
> Grossly overestimated our powers.
>
> (*CP* 465)

For ordinary holiday revelers, the generous hour never existed, and perhaps remains outside the scope of their capability. (In the manuscript Auden seemed a bit surer that it had once existed: "The hours of vision, / The moments of self-forgetfulness have been and gone," he wrote there.)[13] The "Christmas Feast" has also been dismantled and is now "leftovers" to be "warmed up." The holiday may have offered a glimpse of the "Child, however dimly, however incredulously," but it was a child glimpsed through tinsel and mistletoe. The celebration as it now seems to have been experienced was one created by human artifice, and as the poem puts the component parts of Christmas back into cardboard boxes it anticipates its own ending.

Absolute reality, the narrator implies in the closing lines, is outside the realm of the poem. He redefines the locus of spiritual significance as outside the aesthetic bounds of the oratorio, outside the temporal bounds of "the Christmas season," and ultimately outside the secular time being altogether. The present is only an "until," a participial time "being": the "time is noon: / When the Spirit must practice his scales of rejoicing / Without even a hostile audience." In its imperatives to the audience ("Follow Him through the Land of Unlikeness," "Seek Him in the Kingdom of Anxiety"), the final cho-

[13] Holograph manuscript in the Berg Collection, New York Public Library.

rus implies a god that is out there somewhere, off the page, beyond the poem, in a "great city" that is not composed of decorations and tinsel. *For the Time Being* ends with the prediction of a wedding: "Love Him in the World of the Flesh, / And at your marriage all its occasions shall dance for joy." But this "marriage," the union of the soul with God, happens offstage, and when it occurs it will not be in the language of the *Book of Common Prayer*.

The poem concludes, then, with an act of concession, in which it acknowledges that it has not contained true forgiveness and reconciliation within its pages (or on its stage, if the oratorio is performed) but a only tinsel imitation of it. The ultimate reconciliation, when "tutti" sing in God's presence, will not be operatic in form. Distancing himself from a Christmas that was constructed of holly and tinsel and mistletoe, the Narrator explicitly dissociates literature and spectacle from spiritual value. Here the Narrator speaks like Puck or Feste, undoing the fiction of the play in the *plaudite*. In Auden's version of this ancient tradition the poem literally deconstructs itself, puts its pieces into cardboard boxes, and contradicts what it had implied earlier, that its inner scenes represented that ultimate truth of which the familiar world is only a reflection.

The renunciation of one's own importance is the paradigmatic action of *For the Time Being*: what the poem does is what its characters do. The central philosophical event of the entire poem, the poem's concession of its own significance to the greater value of an extrapoetic God, is iterated in the parts of its dramatis personae. For each one, the present moment is a borderline between self-importance and self-forgetfulness. Joseph, the first of the major characters, is interrupted in all his vanity, his tidy clothes and smug confidence:

> My shoes were shined, my pants were clean and pressed,
> And I was hurrying to meet
>   My own true love.
>
> (*CP* 421–22)

Humiliated by the gossip about Mary, he suffers alone "in the jealous trap / Of an empty house." In the first chapter of Matthew, Joseph, "not willing to make her a public example, was minded to put her away privily," but in his sleep the angel persuades him to accept Mary. In Auden's poem the narrator, moving easily from biology to ontology, commands Joseph to revise his notion of identity: "You must learn now that masculinity, / To Nature, is a non-essential luxury." Joseph had been asking for an "Important and elegant proof" that Mary's pregnancy was of divine origin; he is denied such an explanation: "No, you must believe; / Be silent, and sit still."

Joseph must "atone" for the faults of generic man. Just as the poem *For the Time Being* is viewed ultimately as a temporary, artificial set of "decorations" that can be "dismantled" and put in cardboard boxes or burnt, so here masculine identity is presented as a series of theatrical gestures, lies and excuses and symbols and limericks and pornographic pictures, grins and charm and flattering speeches devoid of spiritual value. Masculinity, in short, is deconstructed.

> For the perpetual excuse
> Of Adam for his fall—'My little Eve,
> God bless her, did beguile me and I ate,'
> For his insistence on a nurse,
> All service, breast, and lap, for giving Fate
> Feminine gender to make girls believe
> That they can save him, you must now atone,
> Joseph, in silence and alone. . .
>
> For likening Love to war, for all
> The pay-off lines of limericks in which
> The weak resentful bar-fly shows his sting,
> For talking of their spiritual
> Beauty to chorus-girls, for flattering
> The features of old gorgons who are rich,
> For the impudent grin and Irish charm
> That hides a cold will to do harm . . .

> . . . for gallantry that scrawls
> In idolatrous detail and size
> A symbol of aggression on toilet walls
>
> (*CP* 424–25)

—for all these gestures, Joseph must suffer.

An anti-heroic bridegroom, Auden's Joseph has a "generous hour" inflicted on him from without. Beyond what a later age would label equal rights is the religious equality of God's creatures:

> Joseph and Mary shall be man and wife
> Just as if nothing had occurred.
> There is one World of Nature and one Life;
> Sin fractures the vision, not the Fact. . . .
>
> (*CP* 426)

The fractured vision is Joseph's; the One Life is the totality of created beings. On behalf of Joseph, the Narrator performs a ritualized act of concession to the sacred Coleridgean One Life, a "fact" that lies beyond Joseph's fractured vision: "To choose what is difficult all one's days / As if it were easy, that is faith. Joseph, praise." Charitable love, reconciliation, "man and wife," the One Life, all lie on the other side of the border for Joseph, beyond the limericks and grins and scrawls and deceptions.

Teased by the chorus, silenced by Gabriel, hectored by the Narrator, Joseph does not engage in any serious deliberation. He can only be said to acquiesce, because Auden gives him nothing more to say; Gabriel and the Narrator get all the good lines in "The Temptation of St. Joseph." The star that summons the Wise Men also has a significant speaking role, but it does not scold anyone into self-forgetfulness. The concession it demands is of a more explicitly theological nature. Its appearance in the sky represents "the doom of orthodox sophrosyne," the doom, that is, of conventional wisdom about what is good, self-controlled behavior. Like the narrator with his image of the mirror, the star undermines the familiar and condemns the false without describing the true.

The Wise Men articulate their own reasons for an act of concession. They "follow this star" of their own volition, because they have found their intellectual powers insufficient to make sense of the world. Unlike Joseph, who must "Be silent, and sit still," the Wise Men are quite talkative. For the star demands more than acquiesence; it demands what Auden (in a 1943 speech) called "vocation": "To acknowledge a vocation is, like marriage, to take a vow, to live henceforth by grace of the Absurd, to love for better or for worse, for richer or for poorer, in sickness and in health, until death us do part."[14] If acknowledging a vocation is like making a marriage vow, it requires seeking spiritual value outside oneself. Each Wise Man cheerfully proclaims the triviality of his former ways, characterizing only vaguely what he expects to find after this renunciation: to be "truthful," "living," and "loving" is presumably to discover some ultimate spiritual value, but what that means lies beyond the scope of his present comprehension.

Pausing at the moment of concession, the Wise Men can only deconstruct the secular "faiths" they have abandoned: "scientific materialism," "philosophical idealism," and "liberal rationalism," as Auden wrote in a letter to his father.[15] All these "isms" are "recurrent heathen attempts to reach absolute truth." Here is the Third Wise Man's description of the way his faith in the intellect kept him from loving his neighbor:

> Observing how myopic
> Is the Venus of the Soma,
> The concept Ought would make, I thought,
> Our passions philanthropic,
> And rectify in the sensual eye
> Both lens-flare and lens-coma:
> But arriving at the Greatest Good by introspection

[14] From an unpublished speech in the Auden Collection, McCabe Library, Swarthmore College.

[15] The letter from Auden to his father is in the possession of John Auden and is quoted by permission of the Estate of W. H. Auden, © 1988.

And counting the Greater Number, left no time for affection,
Laughter, kisses, squeezing, smiles:
And I learned why the learned are as despised as they are.
To discover how to be loving now
Is the reason I follow this star.

(*CP* 430)

With the abstract mathematical methods of the Utilitarians the Third Wise Man tried to create some spiritual significance in the world: he attempted, that is, to engineer a wedding feast. But turning other people into integers made it impossible to love them as people: abstractions cannot be kissed or squeezed. The Wise Man—deliberately—does not use the theological language of the star: he has not given up Bentham only to sound like Kierkegaard. Through the unpretentious Gilbert-and-Sullivan-like bounce of a "silly song," the Wise Men advertise their theatricality and their silliness. They follow the star to "discover" significance; they do not know it yet and cannot describe it.

The ritual act of *For the Time Being*, renunciation of one's own spiritual significance, shows most clearly in Herod's refusal to perform it. Herod's monologue (in "The Massacre of the Innocents") not only does not undermine his own worth; it promotes and defends it in every line. The man who is about to order the murder of babies prides himself on the fact that there is "no crime" in the Judea he rules. A "wilderness" luminous with spiritual life,

> where Mongolian idiots are regarded as sacred and mothers who give birth to twins are instantly put to death, where malaria is treated by yelling . . . where the best cuts of meat are reserved for the dead . . . (*CP* 456)

has been replaced by a civilization of inns, soft drinks and sandwiches, parks with decorative swans, bookstores, and allotment gardening. Herod's is a world that obviously ought to be denounced as trivial and insignificant.

The irrational spirituality of "this wretched infant" who is "both God and man" threatens to destroy the urbanity Herod has labored for:

> Justice will be replaced by pity as the cardinal human virtue, and all fear of retribution will vanish. . . . The New Aristocracy will consist exclusively of hermits, bums, and permanent invalids. The Rough Diamond, the Consumptive Whore, the bandit who is good to his mother, the epileptic girl who has a way with animals will be the heroes and heroines of the New Tragedy where the general, the statesman, and the philosopher have become the butt of every farce and satire. (*CP* 459)

Or, as Matthew 5:5 puts it more respectfully, "Blessed are the meek: for they shall inherit the earth." What Herod imagines is a world of forgiveness exaggerated to the point of anarchy: "all fear of retribution will vanish." The "new aristocracy" would come into being through a generous hour: these are the thief and expensive whore and naughty schoolboy of the 1931 epithalamion reborn. Bums and whores and bandits will become "neighbors" one must love, and "Mongolian idiots" will be children of God as much as anyone else. Arrogantly, steadfastly, refusing to acknowledge the unimportance of the artificial world of his own creation, insisting that "Civilization must be saved," Herod (who considers it a mark of progress that the swans in the park are not murdered) will choose to massacre the Innocents.

In his final speech the Narrator calls attention to the triviality of the world from which he speaks and where "we all are,"

> . . . the moderate Aristotelian city
> Of darning and the Eight-Fifteen, where Euclid's geometry
> And Newton's mechanics would account for our experience,
> And the kitchen table exists because I scrub it.
> It seems to have shrunk during the holidays. The streets
> Are much narrower than we remembered; we had forgotten
> The office was as depressing as this.
>
> (*CP* 465)

By speaking in the first person plural, by using colloquial diction, and by referring to ordinary, more or less timeless activities like scrubbing the table and going to the office, the narrator identifies the world he undermines with "our" ordinary world. Because the common world of narrator and implied audience has now been incorporated into the poem, the (actual) audience is not licensed to identify its world with "reality" after the artifice of the poem. "Outside" the poem must therefore become identified with "outside" ordinary life. The shared ordinary world is lacking in spiritual value, though it is redeemable:

> In the meantime
> There are bills to be paid, machines to keep in repair,
> Irregular verbs to learn, the Time Being to redeem
> From insignificance.
>
> (*CP* 456)

To acknowledge that "we" live in a world as trivial as Herod's need not mean that we consider its trivia valuable. It is a world that needs constantly to be redeemed from insignificance. In renouncing its own importance, *For the Time Being* renounces the "importance" of the time being: the temporariness of the poem anticipates the temporariness, the contingent, participial nature of the time "being." The value that makes either significant lies outside its own realm, in a time or place the poem can only describe implicitly as the occasion for which the Spirit must practice his scales of rejoicing.

The Sea and the Mirror

But what exactly *is* implied if the Spirit practices his scales of rejoicing now, in the time being? Vocal rehearsal implies a performance: would a heavenly choir be theatrical? *For the Time Being* anticipates *The Sea and the Mirror* in this respect, that it can call attention to its own artifice but cannot name or locate the realm of superior and ultimate reality. The audience's reality gets described within the poem as a very artificial place indeed. Scrubbing, darning, repairing, practicing—all the activities of the time being imply a world fragmented and frayed, a world of shreds and patches, of stuff that falls apart and has to be put back together again; certainly not a unitary or permanent realm. Both *For the Time Being* and the "time being" are characterized by their artifice and their spiritual incapacities, but the poem does not have much vocabulary for "reality" or spiritual truth. It makes its theological point primarily by having the poem and most of its characters deny themselves spiritual value.

The Sea and the Mirror carries this notion as far as it can go by virtually excluding all vocabulary of the nonartificial. *For the Time Being* does, near the end, refer to "God's Will," but *The Sea and the Mirror* is incapable of referring to a deity directly. He or She is "that Wholly Other Life from which we are separated by an essential emphatic gulf of which our contrived fissures of mirror and proscenium arch . . . are feebly figurative signs" (*CP* 402). The point of this is not simply to show off a Jamesian circumlocutory style, but to dramatize the poem's inability to refer to any extrapoetic reality.[16]

The Sea and the Mirror's preface is subtitled "(The Stage Manager to the Critics)." By beginning his poem with paratheatrical figures, Auden situates it at an apparent border that it never leaves. The poem incorporates characters "outside" art into itself. Insofar as the Stage Manager addresses the audience and mediates between its world and the play's, he has a "role" and is part of the fiction. And who are these "Critics"? Their existence is fictive and hypothetical. The word gives a focus to the Stage Manager's artistic manifesto, but the Critics do not exist within the poem beyond the seven black letters on the white page. And of course, if they had anything to say, they would be Auden's dramatic characters, not "real" critics in the world outside *The Sea and the Mirror*.

The *Postscript* also dramatizes the poem's inability to refer to the extrapoetic world. An echo-song, with "Echo by the Prompter," this lyric shows how a person existing outside the performed text, outside the theatrical fiction, inevitably becomes part of that fiction. The "Prompter" of course becomes one of Auden's characters by being named within Auden's text. The designation of a "prompter" as the person to supply

[16] For another discussion of the style of Caliban's speech, see chapter 1 of this book.

the echo might seem to suggest art's "dependence" on life. But the result is the opposite: the Prompter becomes incorporated into the fiction. He or she is now a necessary part of that fiction. Like a ravenous empire, everything *The Sea and the Mirror* touches it annexes; everything signified becomes, itself, a signifier.

Thus the Stage Manager, the Critics, and the Prompter resemble the genre "commentary": they usually exist *just outside* something artificial, dependent on it and functioning because of it, but not ontologically parts of it. Just as Auden's "commentary" is itself a work of art, and not "life" to *The Tempest*'s "art," so these marginal theatrical figures here turn into dramatis personae in their own right.

How, then, can Auden talk about—or even indicate—spiritual value? If everything the poem mentions turns into itself, it can only refer to "forgiveness," to the secondary mimetic version of the spiritual. By its powerful position at the opening of *The Sea and the Mirror*, the Stage Manager's "Preface" has important ramifications for the rest of the poem. From the backstage space where props are stored and special effects are made, the Stage Manager undermines distinctions between "fake" art and "real" life, and then undermines the ability of language to talk about anything but its own inabilities. His first stanza introduces a very artificial art, a kind of circus, with tightrope-walkers and a "lovely Lady" who is "sawn in half." This is a world that is easy to understand, because it is all so obviously artificial. It is harder to understand "real" existence:

> O what authority gives
> Existence its surprise?
> Science is happy to answer
> That the ghosts who haunt our lives
> Are handy with mirrors and wire. . . .
>
> (*CP* 351)

Attempting to explain the nature of "existence," as opposed to art, the Stage Manager describes it as if it were art, as if we ourselves were a performance managed by "ghosts" who are "handy with mirrors and wire," stage managers themselves, unseen, perhaps subconscious, beings who manipulate us and create the illusion that is our life. (In an early draft of this lyric Auden had the syntax and initial consonants but not the image: "madness," he wrote, inquires "If existence be an illusion / Produced with music and wine." The image takes us back to the wedding feast in *New Year Letter*, but does not fit *The Sea and the Mirror* so well as those tools of the magician's trade, mirrors and wire.)[17] But the explanations of "Science" do not tell us very much: "Our wonder, our terror remains." The appetites of "real life" are fierce and mysterious, and whatever they are hungry for, it is not poetry: the "lion's mouth whose hunger / No metaphors can fill."

"Well," says the Stage Manager, dismissing the indescribability of unartificial existence,

> . . . who in his own backyard
> Has not opened his heart to the smiling
> Secret he cannot quote?
>
> (*CP* 352)

To identify ultimate value with the unquotable is to deny value to the ensuing words of the poem. Implicitly, *The Sea and the Mirror* presents itself as "unsubstantial," trivial, and artificial, like the circus and magic acts of the Stage Manager's first stanza. It is mere metaphors, which cannot satisfy the lion's hunger. It is quotable, and therefore not divine.

Within the frame provided by the paratheatrical characters, the Stage Manager (Preface) and the Prompter (Postscript), each of the poem's main sections undermines the spiritual significance of whatever wedding feast it perceives as having preceded it. Auden's Prospero undermines the resolution of *The Tempest* engineered by Shakespeare's Prospero (part 1: "Prospero to Ariel"). Auden's Antonio undermines that same resolution, and also the smug confidence of Auden's Prospero (part 2: "The Supporting Cast, Sotto Voce"). And Auden's Caliban, in his monologue "to the Audience," undermines

[17] Holograph manuscript in the Berg Collection, New York Public Library.

everything that has preceded him, Shakespeare's play and Auden's "commentary," and then, finally, undermines his own talk to the audience.

Auden's Prospero begins where Shakespeare's left off. He is addressing Ariel ("Stay with me, Ariel, while I pack") and appears to be in his cell on the island. One of his last lines, "Here comes Gonzalo / With a solemn face to fetch me," implies that the whole world of the last pages of Shakespeare's play is still around him. Although Prospero's "space" in *The Sea and the Mirror* looks like his "space" in *The Tempest*, he differentiates himself ontologically as well as chronologically from Shakespeare's Prospero:

> As if I had been on a drunk since I was born
> And suddenly now, and for the first time, am cold sober,
> With all my unanswered wishes and unwashed days
> Stacked up all round my life; as if through
> the ages I had dreamed
> About some tremendous journey I was taking,
>
> . . . .
>
> And now, in my old age, I wake, and this journey really exists,
> And I have actually to take it, inch by inch,
>
> . . . .
>
> Through a universe where time is not foreshortened,
> No animals talk, and there is neither floating nor flying.
> (*CP* 357–58)

That was a drunken, dreaming man, back there; this man, in a time distinctly "after," is sober, awake, in a postmagical world. Whatever happened in *The Tempest*, then, was a matter of floating and flying, in a "universe where time is . . . foreshortened" and animals talk. That era is different from the present because, says Prospero, the present is spiritually significant and the past was not.

Prospero assumes that something resembling a wedding feast did take place in the recent past of *The Tempest*; that all the people temporarily under the spell of his magic are now renewed and redeemed; that he has engineered the kind of grand finale anticipated in *Paid on Both Sides* and *The Dog beneath the Skin*. Yet his language and tone belittle the value of this achievement:

> The extravagant children, who lately swaggered
> Out of the sea like gods, have, I think, been soundly hunted
> By their own devils into their human selves.
>
> (*CP* 356)

Prospero sees the common experience not as a generous hour of forgiveness but as an inflicting of punishment: the "children" who thought they were "gods" have been "hunted." The wedding feast is seen with jaded eyes: Sebastian will be patient with his conscience because "it pays." Stephano is "contracted to his belly, a minor / But a prosperous kingdom." Trinculo "receives, / Gratis, a whole fresh repertoire of stories." "Gratis," like "prosperous" and "it pays," is Prospero's cynical transvaluation of the spiritual into the financial. Miranda and Ferdinand Prospero cannot take seriously: "their eyes are big and blue with love," and Miranda is a "silly lovesick little goose."

From this meting out of rewards and punishments, Prospero himself is separate: "To all, then, but me, their pardons." Prospero uses Cymbeline's famous line dismissively, as if to lump together all the "extravagant children," the naughty ones who needed pardon, and to differentiate them from himself, someone who does not need pardon because he was never an extravagant child. He is a Shakespearean character quoting Shakespeare at others, as if to relegate that silly bunch to mere theatricality: *they* are in a world like the end of *Cymbeline*, whereas *he* has no need of such prizes.

Unlike those poor fools, the extravagant children with their big blue eyes, Prospero himself faces "reality," the silence that is the source of ultimate spiritual truths:

> Can I learn to suffer
> Without saying something ironic or funny
> On suffering? I never suspected the way of truth
> Was a way of silence. . . .
>
> (*CP* 358)

But Prospero's last order to Ariel—whom he has ostensibly freed—asks for sound to fill the silence. What Prospero really wants is a lullaby to comfort and distract him from the disagreeable "way of truth" he has chosen. "Sing, Ariel, sing," he commands,

> Entrancing, rebuking
> The raging heart
> With a smoother song
> Than this rough world,
> Unfeeling god.
>
> (*CP* 359)

Thus as Prospero takes what he calls the "silent passage / Into discomfort," exempt from the need for pardon, he has undermined the spiritual value of everyone else's experience, and exalted the value of his own.[18]

From Antonio's point of view, Prospero's so-called spiritual change is also spurious. Omnipresent and loquacious, Antonio dominates "The Supporting Cast." His poem heads the section, and he inserts himself between the lulls of the other characters' eloquent and sincere speeches to sing a mocking refrain. Each one echoes the lyric it follows only to pervert its imagery and mock its sincerity. He refutes each character's experience of a generous hour. Ferdinand's idealistic love is reduced to lust—

> Hot Ferdinand will never know
> The flame with which Antonio
>   Burns in the dark alone
>
> (*CP* 362)

—and Stephano's acceptance of his stomach and his grief to gluttony:

[18] In "Quitting the Game: Auden's *The Sea and the Mirror*," *Modern Language Quarterly* 41 (1980): 73–87, Dwight Eddins disagrees with my earlier analysis of Prospero ("Artifice and Self-Consciousness"). As is evident from my discussion here, however, I still believe that Auden has created in Prospero an unpleasant, supercilious, and limited character, who claims a religious awareness he does not possess. This interpretation is consistent with Auden's reading of Prospero in two essays in *The Dyer's Hand*, "Balaam and His Ass" and "Music in Shakespeare."

Inert Stephano does not know
The feast at which Antonio
    Toasts One and One alone.

(*CP* 363)

These refrains, in addition, have the effect of separating from one another the people Miranda sees "linked as children in a circle dancing." Coming between them, he ruins the dance.

Prospero had spoken of *The Tempest*'s resolution with disdain as a punishment: Antonio, in elegant terza rima, points out its insubstantiality. "As all the pigs have turned back into men," he begins, implying that whatever transformation occurred was merely external, a bad spell cast by a malicious being. What Prospero has created is only the appearance of a scene of warmth and pardon—"Your grouping could not be more effective"—with special theatrical effects. There was no wedding feast, only a fragile, temporary spectacle. Prospero has given up magic not because he is going to "learn to suffer," but because he has created his grand finale and finished with it.

. . . as long as I choose
To wear my fashion, whatever you wear
Is a magic robe . . .

As I exist so you shall be denied. . . .

(*CP* 361)

Antonio undermines not only the "grouping" Prospero created, but also the "way of truth" Prospero claims to be entering. Prospero had denied spiritual significance to the dramatis personae, excluding himself; Antonio denies it to everyone, excluding *him*self.

The central section of *The Sea and the Mirror* is a diffuse wedding feast with a denial of itself built into it. For the ghost of a wedding feast does indeed haunt "The Supporting Cast, Sotto Voce." Its members are the young lovers, courtiers, servants, and mariners who are drawn to Prospero's magic island and there, in Shakespeare's phrase, "receive a second life." Of these people Auden's Miranda says, "We are linked as children in a circle dancing," an image that suggests the emotional community and aesthetic harmony of the wedding feast. Yet they are both "linked" and separated. Insofar as Antonio's stanzas literally come between the characters, the stanzas separate each character from the surrounding ones. But insofar as the stanzas form a pattern, sound like one another, and virtually constitute a "refrain," the stanzas themselves function as "links" and actually connect the characters. In *The Sea and the Mirror* Auden has his wedding cake and eats it: he includes a wedding feast, and he includes characters who undermine it.

With the exception of Antonio in the section's opening poem, all the characters imply that some kind of grand spiritual transformation has just taken place—whether or not each character feels himself, individually, transformed. Yet each assertion is followed immediately by Antonio's denial of it. Like the kind of optical illusion that is simultaneously the face of a hag and the face of a beauty, "The Supporting Cast" is both a "wedding feast" and the denial of one. The order of the poems is suggestive:

> Antonio + refrain + Ferdinand + refrain + Stephano + refrain + Gonzalo + refrain + Adrian and Francisco + refrain + Alonso + refrain + Master + Boatswain + refrain + Sebastian + refrain + Trinculo + refrain + Miranda + refrain

If Antonio were not there, Ferdinand and Miranda would embrace the whole, linking the characters truly in a circle. His poem looks to her—"Flesh, fair, unique, and you, warm secret that my kiss / Follows into meaning Miranda"—and hers looks to him—"My Dear One is mine as mirrors are lonely"—her line echoing his description of her as "solitude / Where my omissions are." But Antonio *is* there, and so if you do in fact try to "link" the characters as children in a circle dancing, in a circle based on the linear way they appear on the pages, then Antonio clearly comes between Ferdinand and Miranda.

Imagine these as the voices of those highly literary and artificial "blessed, unbamboozled" bridal pairs, "rustic and oppidan," of "City without Walls." What would they say, those decorative, pictorial figures, if they could talk? How do human beings sound when they form such pretty patterns? Well, inevitably, they would deny their own importance as individuals, and emphasize their need of others. A generous hour is a self-forgetful one: how else can egos, singular, eccentric, separate, fit into a design? Thus Ferdinand's vocatives show a clear sequence of ideas from erotic attraction to a metaphysical dependence on Miranda for completeness:

> Flesh, fair, unique, and you, warm secret that my kiss
> Follows into meaning Miranda, solitude
> Where my omissions are. . . .
>
> (*CP* 361)

And both he and Miranda depend on "another tenderness / That neither without either could or would possess," a tenderness that validates and blesses "touch, taste, sight." Miranda defines herself in complementary fashion, though in less philosophical language: "My Dear One is mine as mirrors are lonely": human beings, like mirrors, are blank without another face looking into them. Both poems begin at the point where the ego ends, in a compassionate love, "As the poor and sad are real to the good king." Such ideas form the precondition of all community: Ferdinand's and Miranda's poems seem the inevitable, the necessary, expressions of a bridal pair.

As *New Year Letter*'s wedding feast demonstrated, you do not have to get married to participate in a wedding feast. It can be an intense, temporary harmony of quirky, difficult people, who abandon the "dead-ends of greed and sin" for a community. Stephano's ballade is the low-comic counterpart of Ferdinand's Petrarchan sonnet. His marriage is to his stomach: "Embrace me, belly, like a bride." An apostrophe to one's own stomach hardly suggests self-forgetfulness. Is Stephano still (to use a distinction important to Auden) confusing "hunger" and "love"? Not really: like Ferdinand's, his poem begins with "flesh" but moves beyond the erotic. Buried within his regressive love for the body which is both "child" and "mother," "daughter" and "nanny," is the longing for a generous hour of emotional relief. "Child? Mother? Either grief will do; / The need for pardon is the same." To utter the word "pardon" is at least to approach the wedding feast, with its "warmth and pardon."

Even the word "pardon" lies beyond the comprehension of the Master and Boatswain. Repeatedly, explicitly, they reject the wedding feast. Unbamboozled but not blessed, they speak as if they were in the presence of a wedding feast they did not want to join. They accept disappointment and disillusion as inevitable:

At Dirty Dick's and Sloppy Joe's
  We drank our liquor straight,
Some went upstairs with Margery,
  And some, alas, with Kate;
And two by two like cat and mouse
The homeless played at keeping house.

(*CP* 369)

(Surely the first line's pub names allude to the sad, limited forms of love and hunger indulged in by Master and Boatswain.) To play at keeping house, "two by two," is a perversion of marriage. And when the two are "like cat and mouse" the relationship is not between loving equals but between hunter and prey. Ferdinand's sonnet, moving as it does from "Flesh" to God, shows the direct and necessary connection between sexual love and religious love. Master and Boatswain reject even eros, and so cannot even begin to climb Auden's ladder of love. To reject eros is to reject other people:

There Wealthy Meg, the Sailor's Friend,
  And Marion, cow-eyed,
Opened their arms to me but I
  Refused to step inside;
I was not looking for a cage
In which to mope in my old age.

(*CP* 369)

Where the other characters openly admit their insufficiency (Ferdinand's "omissions," Stephano's "need for pardon"), these two see human relationships as a "cage" trapping the autonomous self. However limited Stephano's awareness may seem after Ferdinand's lofty theological language, he is at least able to articulate his failures and understand that he needs forgiveness. Master and Boatswain deny even the regressive need for liquor and physical love, let alone pardon. They look forward to no healing or redemption, and they have no expectation of any emotional release:

> . . . hearts that we broke long ago
>   Have long been breaking others;
> Tears are round, the sea is deep:
> Roll them overboard and sleep.
>
> (*CP* 369)

For Master and Boatswain, beyond heartbreak and beyond feeling, even sorrow is cut off from expression. The "grief" that Stephano talks about is what the Master and Boatswain evade; they want to roll their tears overboard and drown them. They crave only sleep: not a comforting, healing sleep, but a denial of awareness.

I take the song of Master and Boatswain not as a "denial" of the value of the wedding feast, like Antonio's explicit denials after each song (after all, he has a stanza after their poem too), but as an assertion of it: they acknowledge its existence by affirming their separation from it. Antonio's comment refers to them as "Nostalgic sailors," and in a sense they are: why else do they have round tears to roll overboard? A sorrow is admitted even as the signs of it are rolled overboard. As they define themselves, Master and Boatswain are like Jaques or any sad character who asserts his separation from the happy ending of a Shakespearean comedy. Their tone is perhaps closest to Feste's, when he sings "The rain it raineth every day." They are the "tosspots" who still have drunken heads.

One way or another, then, the members of the "supporting cast," minus Antonio, utter what the "blessed, unbamboozled" bridal pairs of "City without Walls" would say, had they voices. Or they can be imagined as "the erotic" and "the logical," voicing their eccentric but related communal selves. With their distinct verse forms, tones, imageries, and allusions, these characters show the way a community looks, composed as it is of harmonized differences, each (in Eliot's words) "Taking its place to support the others," and "The complete consort dancing together."

It seems superfluous to point out that one way Auden shows the individuality of the members of this community is in the variety of verse forms: "The Supporting Cast, Sotto Voce" is a virtual anthology of poetic forms. These poems—and others by Auden—are often found in handbooks illustrating their various types: sonnet, sestina, villanelle, ballade, and the rest. If one goes back, then, to the bridal pairs of "City without Walls," keeping in mind the whole pattern of dancers, "rustic and oppidan, in a ring dance," the whole pictorial scene, it makes sense that the dancers would speak in a highly artificial mode. "The Supporting Cast" shows this perfectly, both because each individual poem is a classic example of a familiar poetic form, and because the whole bunch taken as a group forms a single virtuoso piece, an anthology of exempla that says, "Hey, look at me! Look at this! One of each kind, no two alike, each a paragon"—like the acrobats waltzing across the tightrope that the Stage Manager describes. That the forms are traditional as well as artificial is yet another way of indicating what a community is: the respect for tradition on the part of the individual talent is another subordination of the self to the whole.

Eliot's description of poetry in *Little Gidding* coincides with Miranda's description of this group, "linked as children in a circle dancing." But Eliot is talking about art; the whole notion of harmony is aesthetic. The wedding feast is a literary idea, as thoroughly artificial as the idea of a poem. It only appears to be about human love; it is really about *claritas*, *integritas*, and *consonantia*. The formality and "literariness" of "The Supporting Cast" undermine it from within, exposing the wedding feast as artificial at the same time as the characters in their sincere, unironic utterances affirm it as genuine.

Prospero calls the reconciled group of characters "extravagant children"; Antonio refers to them as a "grouping," a mere aesthetic effect of Prospero's magic. Caliban goes further than either Prospero or Antonio: to him, *The Tempest* was a play.[19] His section is titled "Caliban to the Audience," and the implications of that title are manifold. It suggests that everything before Caliban, including the preceding sections of *The Sea and the Mirror*, was a theatrical performance. His entire speech, all thirty pages of it, is analogous to the Narrator's final speech in *For the Time Being*: it deconstructs all the preceding parts of the poem. Just as the Narrator referred to broken decorations and cardboard boxes and holly and mistletoe, the artificial means by which we "make" Christmas, so Caliban talks about the other characters as "hired impersonators" and refers throughout his speech to theatrical details: the "laudatory orchid" and "disgusting egg" thrown by members of the audience, the author of the play, the "finally lowered curtain," the whole "artistic contraption."

Caliban's implied audience, like Caliban himself, is on the outside of the lowered curtain. And just as the world of kitchen tables and darning and machines is offered not as "reality" after artifice, but as more unreality, a shadow of something else, so here even the world of the audience turns out to be only another "stage."

For that is Caliban's major breakthrough: that, unlike the dominant speakers of the earlier sections, Prospero and Antonio, he does not arrogate spiritual significance to himself as he denies it to others. He knows he is theatrical too: he undermines his *own* significance. Thus he ultimately achieves, in philosophical form, the self-forgetfulness expressed by Miranda, Ferdinand, Stephano, and other members of the supporting cast. This acknowledgment occurs as Caliban attempts to find some way of talking about life, that is, what is *not* artificial. The way he frames the question is significant: he does not say he wants to describe what is "real." He wants a "large loose image to define the original drama which aroused [the dramatist's] imitative passion"—the "original drama" means what is *not*-drama, what drama is a *mimesis* of, what

[19] On this issue, see also McDiarmid, "Artifice and Self-Consciousness." In parts of my discussion of *The Sea and the Mirror* here I have borrowed phrases and sentences from this article.

in common parlance would be called "life." But as Caliban proceeds to explicate precisely what he means, it becomes clear that he has no language for anything outside art. He wants an *image* for

> . . . the first performance in which the players were their own audience, the worldly stage on which their behaving flesh was really sore and sorry—for the floods of tears were not caused by onions, the deformities and wounds did not come off after a good wash, the self-stabbed heroine could not pick herself up again to make a gracious bow nor her seducer go home to his plain and middle-aged spouse. (*CP* 401)

The image Caliban comes up with to describe this proto-drama, life, is "the greatest grandest opera rendered by a very provincial touring company indeed."

What does this mean? To begin with, it suggests that as Caliban now understands things there is no such thing as "reality" in human life. The image to describe the "original drama" is an "opera." In other words, not only does Caliban not come up with something that seems lifelike, nontheatrical, nonartificial: the "vehicle" of this simile is a "drama" whose artificiality is obtrusively present. This greatest grandest opera is a succession of illusion-breaking incidents. What hired impersonators impersonate is itself a performance, and a bad one:

> Our performance . . . which we were obliged, all of us, to go on with and sit through right to the final dissonant chord, has been so indescribably inexcusably awful. Sweating and shivering in our moth-eaten ill-fitting costumes which with only a change of hat and rearrangement of safety-pins, had to do for the *landsknecht* and the Parisian art-student, bumping into, now a rippling palace, now a primeval forest full of holes, at cross purposes with the scraping bleating orchestra we could scarcely hear for half the instruments were missing and the cottage piano which was filling-out must have stood for too many years in some damp parlour, we floundered on from fiasco to fiasco. (*CP* 401)

Because this is "*our* performance," Caliban now identifies himself as one of the "impersonators," not as the raw life on the other side of the curtain. His talk "to the audience" turns into an "anti-*plaudite*": he and Ariel stand "down stage with red faces and no applause." He does not say, what good actors we were, we only wanted to please; he calls attention instead to "our shame our fear, our incorrigible staginess." To be "stagy" is to be vain, and to be human—to be a shadow, a performer, not an aspect of ultimate reality. "If we shadows have offended": the speech is like a traditional *plaudite* only in its acknowledgment of artifice. Here the audience is included among those who are incorrigibly stagy.

Given that staginess and artifice, poor performances with their moth-eaten costumes and wet pianos, are built into the definition of being human, how can human language signify pardon and not "pardon"? Let us look at the passage in which Caliban alludes to, and asserts that he has come in contact with, a something offstage, not theatrical:

> when our reasons are silenced by the heavy huge derision,—There is nothing to say. There never has been. . . . There is no way out . . . it is at this moment that for the first time in our lives we hear, not the sounds which, as born actors, we have hitherto condescended to use as an excellent vehicle for displaying our personalities and looks, but the real Word which is our only *raison d'être*. . . . we are blessed by that Wholly Other Life from which we are separated by an essential emphatic gulf of which our contrived fissures of mirror and proscenium arch—we understand them at last—are feebly figurative signs . . . it is just here, among the ruins and the bones, that we may rejoice in the perfected Work which is not ours. Its great coherences stand out through all our secular blur in all their overwhelmingly righteous obligation; its voice speaks through our muffling banks of artificial flowers and unflinchingly delivers its authentic molar pardon; its spaces greet us with all their grand old prospect of wonder and width; the working charm is the full bloom of the unbothered state; the sounded note is the restored relation. (*CP* 402–3)

Is Caliban indicating pardon or "pardon"? Has he undergone the kind of spiritual change already undermined by the earlier characters? Our "contrived fissures of mirror and proscenium arch" are "feebly figurative signs" of the separation of human and divine. If, therefore, there is such a thing as a stage, there must be something it is separated from. There must be a theater, an audience, another plane. A stage can only exist by its "difference" from something else. Even if Caliban is stuck onstage, or stuck in *The Sea and the Mirror*, to know that he is in something derivative and contingent is to know that there must be a Something from which his realm derives and on which it depends.

Yet who is to say that the plane from which the stage is separated is not itself another stage, and that separation yet another feebly figurative sign? God, if that is not too simple a word to use, is still experienced as a perfect work of art: his "Work" has "great coherences," and "its spaces greet us with all their grand old prospect of wonder and width."

Nevertheless, unlike the other major voices in *The Sea and the Mirror*, Caliban utters statements that cannot be undermined, because in them he undermines his own authority. Unlike Prospero and Antonio, he performs an act of concession. Even if he is unable to name the power he concedes to, you can hear the concession in his speech. It is the "authentic molar pardon" (a pardon that embraces matter) that enables Caliban to stop talking. The rhythm of Caliban's prose builds up in a crescendo of progressively shorter clauses to the final one with its balanced syntax (the + adjective + noun = the + adjective + noun) and definitive spondaic closure: "the sounded note is the restored relation." He stops being stagy, stops pretending to be absolute, when his relation to the absolute is restored.

Caliban is in the same position as the members of the supporting cast: he speaks as if the pardon he has described is genuine, though someone else sees it as part of a work of art, the penultimate monologue in *The Sea and the Mirror*. Ultimately, *The Sea and the Mirror*, if one applies to it what Caliban has just said, implies that this is "pardon," because of course *The Sea and the Mirror* is the stage on which Auden performs, in a poem its admirers and detractors (if any exist) must admit is as flamboyant, showy, and theatrical a "closet drama" as has ever been written.

An echo-song is the auditory equivalent of a mirror: Ariel's embodies and expresses the dependence of the "shadow" Ariel, art, on substance, the fleshly Caliban to whom the song is addressed:

> Weep no more but pity me,
> Fleet persistent shadow cast
> By your lameness, caught at last,
> Helplessly in love with you,
> Elegance, art, fascination,
>   Fascinated by
>   Drab mortality.
> Spare me a humiliation
>   To your faults be true:
> I can sing as you reply
>   . . . I
>
> (*CP* 403)

This seems fairly straightforward: art, a shadow, depends for its life on human substance, a "lameness" that implies physicality, imperfection, and pain.

Embedded in this spare, elegant language is the metaphor of a marriage, or at least an intense romantic relationship. There is infatuation: "art . . . fascinated by / Drab mortality." The relationship requires fidelity and consistency: "To your faults be true." As long as mortality is drab, imperfect, pained, it will need what art offers. If it were to change and be "untrue," art would be unnecessary and, therefore, humiliated. Like any relationship between human beings, this one entails mutual acceptance and the keeping of promises:

Tempt not your sworn comrade,—only
As I am can I
Love you as you are—
For my company be lonely
For my health be ill:
I will sing if you will cry
. . . I

(*CP* 403)

A rarefied version of "for better for worse . . . in sickness and in health," these lines set the limits of the relationship not between bride and groom, but between art and the life it mirrors. Art should not be "tempted" to become more than it is; it is only a mirror, not substance. Only when acknowledged as merely a shadow or reflection can it love life in its imperfection. "For my company be lonely" suggests both the very human desire, "miss me," and the philosophical statement that art comes into being when ordinary life appears to be missing something. For art to be alive and healthy, people must in some sense be "ill." "I will sing if you will cry" because Ariel is Caliban's "sworn comrade," and reacts with sympathy to his emotions; and because the song that is art arises from human unhappiness. (The phrase "sworn comrade" is a suggestive one: it might also characterize what Auden felt he was to Chester Kallman, and Kallman to him. They could not be "married," yet Auden felt that they had made "vows" of commitment to one another. Auden was certainly helplessly in love with Kallman, and Kallman was certainly true to his faults.)

The self's dependence on something outside for completeness is brilliantly embodied in the actual syllable of the echo, the "I" which is the sworn comrade's response, like "reply," "cry," and "sigh"—all words that describe different modes of response from one's lover—as well as the other person's statement of his individuality, his personal pronoun. Yet this "echo-song" calls attention to art's inability to maintain any intimacy with the world beyond itself, because this song is a *postscript*. By definition a postscript comes after something written: how could it be sung? The "I," like the Prompter, is something apparently outside *The Sea and the Mirror* that is in fact built into it. Ariel's concession, like Caliban's, can only be a self-effacing acknowledgment of limitation, not a concession *to* anything.

And so the answer to Emily Brontë's question is Yes.

And am I wrong to worship where
Faith cannot doubt nor Hope despair
Since my own soul can grant my prayer?
Speak, God of Visions, plead for me
And tell why I have chosen thee.

(*CP* 349)

Yes, Brontë (as quoted in the epigraph to *The Sea and the Mirror*) is "wrong" to worship the God of art, her own imagination, her "Darling Pain." This "radiant angel" for whom she cast the world away is a muse. Although Brontë's poem (which Auden anthologized several years later in the Viking portable *Victorian and Edwardian Poets*) is couched in religious language, as if she were talking about a traditional conversion, the "God" she worships is clearly one she has created, "Since my own soul can grant my prayer." This is a God who can no more be "outside" herself or her writings than the real Word can exist outside Caliban's talk, which is of course Auden's writing. Brontë's rhetorical question should be seen as another of the texts on which *The Sea and the Mirror* provides a "commentary." Her unironic faith in the imagination's ability to *be* God is challenged by each of the subsequent speakers, beginning with the Stage Manager and his unquotable deity and ending with Ariel and the unsingable echo-song.

"We live in a new age," Auden announced in 1949, "in which the artist neither can have . . . a unique heroic importance nor believes in the Art-God enough to desire it" (*EF* 150). If you take *The Sea and the Mirror* seriously, you know that all its characters are stuck in the poem, and that the poem's only raison d'être is to undermine the spiritual significance of all art. True pardon and true worship inevitably lie outside all language: art has nothing to do with them. But like the circus described by the Stage Manager, art makes the aged catch their breath, makes the wounded cry, and makes the dear little children laugh—remarkable powers to have, even if they are not spiritual.

CHAPTER FOUR

Apologies for Poetry: Poems 1948–1973

> One might say that for Truth the word "silence" is the least inadequate metaphor, and that words can bear witness to silence only as shadows bear witness to light. . . . The only witness to the living God . . . which poetry can bear is indirect and negative.
>
> —Auden, "Words and the Word," *Secondary Worlds*

"BUT PERHAPS you think poems are as foolish / as most poets," Auden remarks in "Epistle to a Godson," deprecating the previous eighty lines of his poem and implicitly apologizing for whatever follows (*EG* 6, 1969). The "epistle" to Auden's godson Philip Spender devotes most of its time to explaining why it cannot be written: its author, says the poem, has no authority. Auden undermines his own status from the beginning: "who am I to avouch for any Christian / baby, far less offer ghostly platitudes / to a young man?" And, farther on, "*I speak from experience*, how could I / say that to you . . . ?" And later: "who can / issue proper instructions?" The godson is granted more intelligence than the speaker grants himself: "You don't need me to tell you what's / going on."

After seventeen stanzas of self-denigration Auden finally seems about to make what his poem might consider a definitive statement; finally he seems about to "write" the epistle: "what should we write to give . . . nourishment, / warmth and shelter . . . ?" But then he immediately undermines his brief attempt (the only unqualified five lines he has uttered) by introducing the possibility that Philip Spender thinks poems and poets are foolish. The "worldly maxims" Auden closes with are not the slightest bit worldly: one is a religious statement ("*Be glad your being is unnecessary*"); the others borrow their imperative force from the Red Queen's confident authority: "*turn your toes out as you walk, dear, / and remember who you are, a Spender.*"

The note of benign tolerance ("All pleasures / come from God") and whimsical mock-authority the poem ends on does not altogether counteract the poem's undermining of itself. Auden sounds more respectful of Philip Spender's pastimes than of his own. The subject of the poem appears to be the impossibility of *anyone's* giving advice to anyone else; the Red Queen's advice stands in for all that is arbitrary when the older generation addresses the younger (Auden does not quote her first maxim, "Speak in French when you ca'n't think of the English for a thing—"). All purportedly "serious" pursuits must be seen as play, Auden's poems as well as Philip Spender's philosophy, and all derive from God. The poem bows off modestly, mocking the ambitions it has already deprecated, and deferring to a Greater Authority.

Deference, apology, self-deprecation—these become ritual gestures in Auden's later poetry. The lyrics written after 1948 are definitely "post-Caliban": each assumes that all poems, itself not excluded, are silly and trivial, examples of "incorrigible staginess" that need to be apologized for and forgiven. This notion is not "discovered" within the poem, as it was in *The Sea and the Mirror*: the poem takes it for granted. The poem is the stage on which the poet shows off: at the end of his "play" he speaks a kind of anti-*plaudite*, in which he does not ask for applause but asserts that the poem has been silly and insignificant, acknowledges his own weakness, and defers to some greater power. Auden humbles himself, or some poet stand-in, before limestone, Clio, Gaea, the Mezzogiorno, Terminus, God, and even before other poets: Chaucer, Langland, Dunbar, Hardy, Frost, Graves, MacNeice. The sounded note is the tone of perpetual apology.

In a number of poems, in fact, the poet, or the idea of a poet, is abruptly introduced into the poem, near the end, so the poem ends in a pose of self-deprecation or self-admonition. "Hunting Season" (a somewhat unsubtle poem that reads like a vegetarian manifesto) begins "A shot," and shows sundry results of the noise that signifies a bird's death. Embracing lovers pull apart in surprise, and the poet realizes that it is mealtime:

Down in the startled valley
   Two lovers break apart:
He hears the roaring oven
   Of a witch's heart;
Behind his murmurs of her name
She sees a marksman taking aim.

Reminded of the hour
   And that his chair is hard,
A deathless verse half done,
   One interrupted bard
Postpones his dying with a dish
Of several suffocated fish.

(*SA* 40)

The yoking of poet and lovers is ominous; this must be a narcissistic, hyperbolic poet. At the gunshot, each lover reads the other one as predatory, and the poet is reminded to prey on his lunch, seen not as a tuna salad sandwich but as recently murdered creatures. This cruel person is described in mock-grandiloquent language as a "bard" to indicate his own sense of his importance, and his poem is a "deathless verse"—deathless, of course, because it can never be shot. The structure of the poem is an implicit progression, indicating increasingly predatory, self-centered behavior: hunter, lovers, bard. You might think of a poet as peacefully scribbling away while other people kill, but this "bard" lives, like everyone else, by the sacrifice of natural creatures.

The "humbling" of the poet can involve deference as well as castigation: in "Homage to Clio" the muse of history is praised as a forgiving, maternal Madonna of mercy:

> I have seen
> Your photo, I think, in the papers, nursing
> A baby or mourning a corpse. . . .
>
> (*HC* 5)

Loving and uncritical, Clio is another manifestation of the Virgin—or Elizabeth Mayer, for that matter. Auden prays to her, "forgive our noises / And teach us our recollections," and ends on the typical note of self-deprecation:

> Approachable as you seem,
> I dare not ask you if you bless the poets,
> For you do not look as if you ever read them,
> Nor can I see a reason why you should.
>
> (*HC* 6)

As the merciful and silent muse, Clio cannot say anything for herself in this poem, of course; she exists as the fiction of a talkative poet in a poem where "noises" require forgiveness. The poet introduces his own vocation only to condemn it through a form of *praeteritio*. In true Ciceronian fashion he specifies what he does not wish to state: "I dare not ask you if you bless the poets." And, having not-asked his question, he approvingly announces that this wonderfully merciful goddess ignores the work of people like him. Poetry is mere noise, trivial, naughty, stagy, and why would silent, loving Clio pay any attention to it?

This is a coy, teasing self-reference: the naughty boy ostentatiously reveals and conceals his naughtiness, indicating both that he knows he is naughty and that he wants Mother to forgive him. Clio does not need this attribute—the not-reading of poetry—to magnify her; Auden mentions "the poets" in order to bow deferentially off the stage of the poem. Perhaps, as in "Precious Five," Auden is "Telling for Her dear sake / To whom all styles belong / The truth She cannot make."

Like the bard lunching on fish, the kind of poet Auden's

allusions depict is not much like W. H. Auden. In 1950, in the epigraph to *Nones*, Auden characterized his particular variety of post-romantic style: "the wry, the sotto-voce, / Ironic and monochrome." Nevertheless he seems haunted by the danger of being loud-voiced and serious. "Cattivo Tempo" (1949) describes the "imp" who ruins poetry, making "The manner arch / The meaning blurred, / The poem bad." Auden warns, "Beware of him, poet." Nineteen years later "Ode to Terminus" praises the divinity who counteracts this imp, the "God of walls, doors and reticence." Terminus is needed when the mind "discarding rhythm, punctuation, metaphor . . . sinks into a driveling monologue." Worshipping Terminus and his "grace," Auden recites what he has learned,

> that abhorred in the Heav'ns are all
> self-proclaimed poets who, to wow an
> audience, utter some resonant lie.
>
> (*CWW* 99)

Ouch! A spanking for me, in case I have said something bad or hyperbolic! Auden bows off as usual, apologizing for the behavior of his tribe.

And so, in "Ode to Gaea," he returns from the mysterious absolute of Heaven's view of earth to his own trivial perspective, where

> Good-manners will ask easy riddles like "Why are all
> The rowdiest marches and the
> Most venemous iambics composed
>
> By lame clergymen?", will tell no tales which end in worse
> Disaster than that of the tipsy poet who cursed
> A baby for whom later
> He came to sigh. . . .
>
> (*SA* 57)

Earth is a place, that is, where loud-mouthed poems compensate for physical weakness, and where poets are drunken blithering idiots, angry or infatuated. Is this Auden? It does not sound like him, but these are the obligatory self-castigations, the ritual apologies of the derivative to the absolute.

Even when he praises other poets, Auden must do so at his own expense. Provisionally, for the duration of the poem, *other* poets assume the role of divinity. "Chaucer, Langland, Douglas, Dunbar," Auden apostrophizes, how did you manage "to write so cheerfully" and self-forgetfully, when modern poets are "petrified by their gorgon egos"? The final note of reverence is the ritual self-deprecation:

> I would gladly just now be
>
> turning out verses to applaud a thundery
> jovial June when the judas-tree is in blossom,
> but am forbidden by the knowledge
> that you would have wrought them so much better.
>
> (*EG* 58)

In one of his final poems, published posthumously, Auden defers to all his predecessors. No Bloomian Oedipus killing off these precursors, Auden belittles himself before the poetic feet of Hardy, Thomas, Frost, Yeats, Graves, Brecht, Kierkegaard, Williams, Lewis, Horace, and Goethe. Before this pantheon, in a classic *veneratio poetarum*, Auden utters "A Thanksgiving":

> Fondly I ponder You all:
> without You I couldn't have managed
> even my weakest of lines.
>
> (*TYF* 37)

Yeats of all people, whom Auden had on occasion *blamed* for his "weakest of lines"! Auden humbles himself out of poetic existence here.

Even the poets "thanked" for being Auden's later models, Goethe and Horace, are themselves deprecated in other poems. Auden praises the openness, immediacy, and sexuality of the Mezzogiorno at the expense of the self-conscious Northerners who escape there:

We are not bad, but hopeless as tutors: Goethe,
Tapping Homeric hexameters
On the shoulder blade of a Roman girl, is
(I wish it were someone else) the figure

Of all our stamp. . . .

(*HC* 81)

Here is the revered Goethe at a most embarrassing moment, caught in the act of writing poetry and confusing it with sex.[1] And the poem written in what appears to be homage to "The Horatians" ends with words of modest self-deprecation, which Auden puts in Horace's mouth:

As makers go,
compared with Pindar or any

of the great foudroyant masters who don't ever
amend, we are, for all our polish, of little
stature, and, as human lives,
compared with authentic martyrs

like Regulus, of no account. We can only
do what it seems to us we were made for, look at
this world with a happy eye
but from a sober perspective.

(*CWW* 28)

Is this praise? The great Horatian art, with its control and balance and concinnity, is presented apologetically. Horace's own proud statement of his poetry's worth ("*Exegi monumentum aere perennius*") Auden dismisses earlier: "You thought well of your Odes, Flaccus, and believed they / would live," but this is what you would *really* say. We are insignificant, compared with more flamboyant poets, and "of no account" at all compared with those who sacrifice their lives for

[1] The allusion is to Goethe's *Römische Elegien V*: "Oftmals hab ich auch schon in ihren Armen gedichtet / Und des Hexameters Mass leise mit fingernder Hand / Ihr auf den Rücken gezählt" (Often I have even written poetry while in her arms and gently counted out the beat of the hexameter with my fingers on her back).

their countries. If the final assertion is self-referential, that "sober perspective" entails a humbling of oneself. The Horatians would not be "sober" if they thought they were more important than Regulus. And so they cannot even be proud of their sobriety; it must be presented as a concession: "We can only. . . ." This "sober perspective" is Horace Audenized.[2]

In lines that have since been often quoted, Auden announced in one of his lectures as Professor of Poetry at Oxford that the "impulse to create a work of art is felt when . . . the passive awe provoked by sacred beings or events is transformed into a desire to express that awe in a rite of worship or homage. . . . In poetry the rite is verbal; it pays homage by naming" (*DH* 57). The part of that rite Auden did not describe is the corollary of homage, the worshiper's self-denigration. In Auden's later poetry, his most common means of attributing spiritual significance to what he is praising is to deny it to himself. And Auden denies it to himself *as poet*, undermining the significance of the very rite of homage. Whatever the "impulse" to create these works of art may have been, their *subject* always ends up being the poet's incapacity to say anything worthy of the spiritual absolutes he can only name.[3]

[2] Some of this modesty Auden does inherit from Horace: see, for example, *Odes* 1.20.1–2, *Epistles* 1.5.1–2, and Horace's frequent use of understated verbs such as *dico* and *loquor* for his profession as poet. Professor John Hunt of the Classics Department of Villanova University has kindly discussed this issue with me.

[3] Both Samuel Hynes and Stanley Hopper have suggested to me the religious importance for Auden of poetry-as-praise, citing many poems ("In Praise of Limestone," "Precious Five," and others) as well as Auden's comments in "Making, Knowing and Judging" (*DH* 32–60). In that essay Auden announces, with more than usual fanfare, "there is only one thing that all poetry must do; it must praise all it can for being and for happening" (*DH* 60). That resonant description fits only a small handful of Auden's poems, the best of them written in the early 1950s, around the time of the essay. My reading of the poems I discuss in this chapter suggests that Auden writes such poems as much to undermine their author as to praise their subject. "Precious Five" (a poeticizing of the last sentence of "Making, Knowing and Judging") seems to me praise of "Barnaby," that is, an unselfconscious sensual self. Literature can command praise ("Praise, tongue, the Earthly Muse," "*Bless what there is for being*"), but is not, itself, similarly praiseworthy. Auden dares not

I

"The Shield of Achilles" (1952) offers the major statement of the aesthetics of postwar Auden. Its subject is what art cannot do; the poem dramatizes its own incapacities. An intertextual reading, by way of introduction to the poem, bears out this definition of its subject: "The Shield of Achilles" rereads its sources by severely qualifying their assertions of art's significance.

The first comment is of course on the *Iliad*. Many of Auden's critics, eager for simple contrasts, forget that there were *two* cities on the original Homeric shield.[4] *One* of the cities has scenes of "marriages" and "festivals" and arbitration and civic order, "But around the other city were lying two forces of armed men / shining in their war gear."[5] The original shield even includes "two herdsman . . . playing happily on pipes" who are unaware of an ambush, and are soon killed.[6] Homer is no naive pastoralist, and Auden's commentary on Homer is subtler than it has been given credit for. Auden does not reread the "heroic" world of Homer as the "barbaric" modern world, nor would Auden call what Thetis looks for "the classical virtues" of Homer.[7]

Auden rereads Homer insofar as he emphasizes the *inabilities* of art. Homer's pleasure in the shield is not in its arcadian beauty but in its inclusiveness: it has one city *and another* and then also a field and a vineyard and a herd of oxen and a dancing-floor. Each of these is a separate, autonomous scene. In the Greek a series of rhetorically parallel sentences (*ain de*, *ain de*)

---

ask Clio (in "Homage to Clio") if she blesses the poets. For a different point of view, see Stanley Hopper, "W. H. Auden and the Circumstance of Praise," *Journal of the American Academy of Religion* 43, no. 2 (June 1975), 135–52.

[4] See Spears, *Poetry of W. H. Auden*, 315; Fuller, *Reader's Guide*, 228; and Johnson, *Man's Place*, 170.

[5] *Iliad* 18.509–10, trans. Richmond Lattimore (Chicago and London, 1951, 1961), 388–89.

[6] *Iliad* 18.525–26, trans. Lattimore, 389.

[7] John Blair, *The Poetic Art of W. H. Auden* (Princeton, 1965), 82; Fuller, *Reader's Guide*, 228.

creates the impression of an accumulation of scenes.[8] The fact that—last of all—Hephaistos forges Ocean around the rim of the shield implies that the scenes truly constitute a microcosm. The finished shield is *mega te stibaron te*, great and strong, and Homer in no way qualifies it.[9] Auden, as we shall see, reminds his readers in almost every line of what the shield cannot do: never does he call it great and strong.

The scenes on Auden's shield come also, I believe, by way of the Grecian Urn. For there is a poem that does state what art cannot do, and a poet who hovers over the fair youth and tells him "thou canst not leave / Thy song," tells the lover, "never, never canst thou kiss," and the trees that they cannot shed their leaves, and imagines the town *not* on the urn and informs it, "thy streets for evermore / Will silent be." Yet in spite of these qualifications Keats does still attribute to the urn one significant power: it is a "friend to man." Auden makes no such statement of his shield: at the end of his poem, the artist hobbles off without comment, and the audience cries out in dismay. Nothing is said about the shield's friendliness.[10]

Auden's revision of both sources has nothing to do with the kind of scene depicted, but with the philosophical issue of the poem's self-commentary. Homer's shield is comprehensive; Ocean runs around it as it does around the actual globe. Keats's urn is inorganic, a passionless "Cold Pastoral"; it does advertise its own inabilities, yet the poet nevertheless labels it a "friend" and attributes to it the teasing aphorism, "Beauty is truth, truth beauty." Auden's shield reveals by synecdoche the way art deconstructs itself, so that it does not only advertise its inabilities; they constitute its subject.

Like the end of "Homage to Clio," in which Auden does not dare to ask Clio if she reads the poets, "The Shield of Achilles" uses *praeteritio* to show what it cannot show. The poem is a parable of the relation between art and its audience. It is struc-

[8] *Iliad* 18, 490, 541, 550, 561, 573, 587, 590, 607.

[9] *Iliad* 18, 609.

[10] See also Joost Daalder, "W. H. Auden's 'The Shield of Achilles' and Its Sources," *Journal of the Australasian Universities Language and Literature Association* 42 (1974): 186–98.

tured by a series of escalating demands (on the part of the audience) and escalating denials (on the part of the shield). With each of the three sets of exchanges, more of life is viewed as undepictable.

Thetis is the last of Auden's demanding mothers: like John Nower's and Michael Ransom's mothers, she is implicated in her son's death. It is she who goes to Hephaestos for a shield, implicitly sanctioning the death in battle of "Iron-hearted man-slaying Achilles / Who would not live long." As the audience for a work of art, Thetis can also be numbered among Auden's naive aesthetes, like the first speaker of "O what is that sound that so thrills the ear" and the lover in "As I walked out one evening." She is someone who desires "beauty" and assumes it is "truth." Her mind does not go beyond the dichotomy of the pretty and the ugly; she must be shocked into moral awareness. Her demands are simple and absolute.

The clearest example of the way the subject of "The Shield of Achilles" is art's own inabilities occurs in the third contrast between what Thetis looks for and what the shield shows her:

She looked over his shoulder
   For athletes at their games,
Men and women in a dance
   Moving their sweet limbs
Quick, quick, to music,
   But there on the shining shield
His hands had set no dancing-floor
   But a weed-choked field.

A ragged urchin, aimless and alone,
   Loitered about that vacancy; a bird
Flew up to safety from his well-aimed stone:
   That girls are raped, that two boys knife a third,
   Were axioms to him, who'd never heard
Of any world where promises are kept
Or one could weep because another wept.

(*SA* 37)

Thetis is looking for something like the scene of warmth and pardon Auden describes in "City without Walls," an aesthetically pleasing and emotionally harmonious vision of reconciliation between men and women, and between human beings and the universe. The scene Thetis describes is one in which by long literary and iconographic tradition aesthetic qualities signify spiritual ones. Thetis wants transcendent play, human activities elevated to a sublime spirituality.

The lines in the following "shield" stanza describe primarily what cannot be on the shield. It is certainly possible to show a ragged urchin alone in a weed-choked field and a bird in the sky above him: but how could a shield show "axioms" in a child's mind, and how indeed could it show *what he has never heard of*? These notions exist in an abstract and hypothetical dimension that cannot be made pictorial; and so, the poem implies, the spiritual cannot be depicted in poetry or in any work of art. Just as dimensions are missing in the visual arts, a dimension is missing in language. Why describe in language ("Were axioms to him, who'd never heard . . .") what cannot possibly be on the shield, if not to dramatize that the qualities he has never heard of, commitment and sympathy, can never be in a work of art?

If art is not wish-fulfillment, as Thetis assumes, what is it? Auden in the 1950s would say, a means of disenchantment, through which our expectations for the absolute are answered with the contingent and derivative. If art's subject is always its own incapacities, then it will always disenchant those who come to it seeking the fulfillment of their wishes. The notion of disenchantment is built into an art that dramatizes what it cannot do. In the juxtaposition of the wish to see "Men and women in a dance / Moving their sweet limbs" with the *absence* from the shield of promise-keeping and sympathy, Auden takes the "meaning" of the scene Thetis wanted, and demonstrates its undepictability. Only through *praeteritio* does Auden introduce into the poem the notions of promise-keeping and sympathy.

The final pair of Thetis-shield stanzas only dramatizes the poem's subject more emphatically than the earlier pairs. The central idea of undepictability exists throughout the poem. In the poem's opening stanza, Thetis expresses the naive audience's wish to see "Marble well-governed cities," that is, scenes in which moral values (well-governed) are signified by aesthetic qualities (marble). Thetis wants art to be artistic and "literary"; her expectations are voiced in pseudo-Homeric formulas, "ships upon untamed seas." What Thetis has created in her imagination, the poem uncreates, describing not what *is* on the shield but what is *not* on it: "A plain *without* a feature. . . . *No* blade of grass, *no* sign of neighborhood, / *Nothing* to seat and *nowhere* to sit down" (emphasis added). An absence—like the compassion the urchin *has never heard of*—is undepictable.

The second stanza here dramatizes qualities that could not be forged on a shield: the "voice" without a face and its "dry and level" tones as well as the *absence* of cheering and discussion. The final lines of this set are reminiscent of Keats's little town: "They marched away enduring a belief / Whose logic brought them, somewhere else, to grief." How can this vague "somewhere else," the doom to which the five hundred thousand people are marching, be part of the shield? How can a visual art show people marching away "enduring a belief"? Or how show the logical (though not-yet-existing) outcome of that belief? The absent visual dimension on the shield signifies the absent spiritual dimension of art, which, "The Shield of Achilles" implies, is limited to telling you by means of *praeteritio* what it cannot tell you.

Thetis's naiveté is not necessarily about "life"; we do not know what she thinks about that. We only know what she expects art to be, what she "looked over" Hephaistos's shoulder to see. Thetis expects that art will be aesthetically pleasing, and that some form of moral and spiritual value will be somehow "built in" to its beauty; that "marble" and "well-governed" will be synonymous. The harshness of the denial reflects the excess of the wish.

In the second pair of expectations and disenchantments, Thetis's wishes escalate, and hence so do the "shield's" denials. Moving from the civic and social to the religious realm,

Thetis wants to see "ritual pieties." Her concern is not with the spiritual attitude of the participants but the ceremonial aspects: she wants "White flower-garlanded heifers, / Libation and sacrifice." Thetis must have been reading Homer or Virgil (or "Ode on a Grecian Urn") to have such specific notions of what is involved in ritual pieties. She wants *mere* ceremony, but she herself is not aware of its "mereness."

The shield's answer is, again, a comment on art: what you want, it implies, would be empty of spiritual significance. Art is not the same as religion. The "rites" depicted in art would be without significance. Anything in art is arbitrary: hence the "arbitrary" spot enclosed by the barbed wire. What you are expecting, the shield suggests, implies that there is no difference between art's version of a "ritual piety" and the actual ritual. The location of a ceremony in art would not be traditional and sacred. Art would not care whether it was white heifers or pale people who were being sacrificed. *Art has no feelings*. The people in charge of such a fabricated ritual piety might as well be "bored," because they do not have insides. You would have a ritual on the surface only, a ritual drained of value.

What is truly significant in any ritual piety is undepictable, a spirituality beyond the capabilities of art. Auden deliberately comments on the shield's own "anti-ritual" in ways that the shield could not possibly comment. How could a design on metal say that people about to be executed "could not hope for help" and that they "lost their pride / And died as men before their bodies died"? This is an area art cannot touch, cannot talk about, yet this is precisely the area of spiritual significance. Auden creates a scene so obviously undepictable visually in order to dramatize what art cannot do. Art cannot express sympathy: the most it can do is imply that it is unable to express sympathy.[11]

[11] I therefore disagree with Claude J. Summers, who reads the poem more didactically, saying that it "bitterly indicts ancient and modern failures of love" and also "prescribes Agape as a religious and political solution to the contemporary malaise" (" 'Or One Could Weep Because Another Wept': The Counterplot of Auden's 'The Shield of Achilles'," *Journal of English and Ger-*

Just as the poem makes comments that the shield could not possibly make, so there exists outside the poem an infinite range of comments that literature cannot make. And *this* is the poem's subject. Thetis as parabolic audience has unexamined and absolute expectations of what art should reveal: it should be pretty, of course, a kind of Blakean Innocence where conflict is not known. It should be a series of appealing nouns—vines, olive trees, cities, ships, heifers, athletes, dancers—arranged in attractive scenes, without commentary. These scenes should have vaguely "good" suggestions about them: civic order, traditional religion, spiritual harmony. The shield as parabolic work of art disturbs Thetis's expectations, disappointing her item by item and asserting its inability to make spiritually valuable comments. If the shield is an example, and it is, the only subject of art is its inability to comment on just those experiences and feelings most important to humankind: suffering, compassion, love.

In the last stanza of "The Shield of Achilles," the artist himself appears for the first time. He is "thin-lipped": he has nothing to say. His work of art says it all for him: why should he talk? He hobbles away because he is finished: he has made his shield and that is all he can do. He cannot stand around chatting with the audience he has just disappointed. After he hobbles off Thetis "Cried out in dismay," but the audience's reaction is beyond the concern of the artist. His role is not to comfort her but to create. His creations speak. And what business has Thetis anyway to expect spiritual niceties to please her "Iron-hearted man-slaying" son? A naive attitude to art betrays an unexamined attitude to the part of the world that is not art also. But the artist does not know that and does not interfere with the realities of her world. Teasingly, defiantly, he embodies in his art his inability to talk about the spiritually significant.

---

manic Philology 8, no. 2 [April 1984], 215). Summers also calls the "poem's real subject . . . the plight of the individual in the contemporary world reflected on the shield" (220). I am, of course, in agreement with Summers when he observes that "The Shield of Achilles" is "by no means simply an ironic or anachronistic retelling of a classical story" (218).

II

Toward the end of "In Praise of Limestone" the poet, as such, makes his appearance. Just at the moment when the poem suggests that limestone may not be childishly innocent but "backward and delapidated" and seedy, a place to outgrow, limestone begins to show its strength. It

> . . . calls into question
> All the Great Powers assume; it disturbs our rights. The poet,
> Admired for his earnest habit of calling
> The sun the sun, his mind Puzzle, is made uneasy
> By these solid statues which so obviously doubt
> His antimythological myth.
>
> (*N* 15)

This is the first of those occasions, so prevalent in Auden's later poetry, when the worshiper introduces himself *as poet* in order to denigrate himself and praise a divinity. The two judgments are simultaneous and inseparable: the very moment that first shows limestone's moral authority reveals the poet as shamefaced, silly, undignified.

"In Praise of Limestone" undermines its own significance not by showing how poetry fails to make grand absolute spiritual statements, but by showing how poetry is, in origin, a deviation from value. "In Praise of Limestone" is not a parable: it is an aetiology of art, art's own autobiography. Its cheerful tone derives from its acceptance of itself as benign play, and its attribution of spiritual force to limestone. *New Year Letter* is the dominant ancestor of "In Praise of Limestone": Elizabeth Mayer's *solificatio*, the warmth she spreads throughout the universe, is here projected onto a landscape of rounded slopes and chuckles and "short distances and definite places: / What could be more like Mother . . . ?" The guilty speaker of *New Year Letter*, who worshipfully directed his missive to the nearest Beatrice, appears early on as "her son . . . the nude young male . . . displaying his dildo," then as the boy competing with his brothers, then the self-centered poet, and, finally, as the confessional "I." As son to mother, as sinner to merciful intermediary, so poet to limestone.

"In Praise of Limestone" divides the world into two parts, limestone and everything else. The two terms are equivalent to "Nature" and "History" as Auden defines them in his later essays and in most of his later poems, particularly those in the volume *Homage to Clio* (*DH* 61–71). Limestone encompasses the entire created world, rocks, water, what is before *homo faber* fabricates anything; the poem's even, regular movements, alternating lines of eleven and thirteen syllables, are a tribute to the regularity of natural rhythms, like breathing or the seasons. As civilization evolves gradually from nature, so child is differentiated from mother. With each line of "In Praise of Limestone" the process of differentiation is accomplished: each line signifies a new stage of development, as the poem reenacts the development of self-consciousness, from sensual awareness (touch, rounded slopes; smell, fragrance of thyme; sound, springs chuckling; sight, short distances) to Mother to "brothers" to "rivals" to the introspective and alienated "solitude that asks and promises nothing."

Parallel to this ontogenetic development is the evolution of culture, as it rises out of limestone gradually:

From weathered outcrop
To hill-top temple, from appearing waters to
Conspicuous fountains, from a wild to a formal vineyard,
Are ingenious but short steps that a child's wish
To receive more attention than his brothers, whether
By pleasing or teasing, can easily take.

(*N* 13)

The child's "works are but / Extensions of his power to charm," artistic efforts designed to get attention: thus a later, more self-conscious version, the impulse to "ruin a fine tenor voice / For effects that bring down the house."

Art, then, is a form of pleasing and teasing and naughtiness, a sign of individuation and separation from loving Mother limestone. Grown up, the naughty children leave limestone and its affectionate embrace for lonelier lives, as saints, Caesars, or isolated romantic voyagers. Out in the big busy world, they look back on limestone as backward and seedy.

It is at this point in the poem that limestone begins to acquire spiritual authority, changing from a warm loving Mommy to a more theological Love. The poet himself is caught in all his pride, deifying himself ("calling . . . his mind Puzzle"), as the capital letter suggests, and depriving nature of any divine power: he calls the sun "the sun," not Apollo. His myth is "antimythological" because he is too knowing and sophisticated to believe in Naiads and Dryads and Daphne and Syrinx. Statues make him uneasy because they are so physical; if, as the poem suggests several lines later, they are "Innocent athletes," their nakedness disturbs his intellectuality.

In one of the most complex instances of self-deprecation in all his poetry, Auden humbles the first-person speaker of "In Praise of Limestone" for his failure to worship limestone, the natural world that the God of Genesis saw and called "good."

> I, too, am reproached, for what
> And how much you know. Not to lose time, not to get caught,
> Not to be left behind, not, please! to resemble
> The beasts who repeat themselves, or a thing like water
> Or stone whose conduct can be predicted, these
> Are our Common Prayer, whose greatest comfort is music
> Which can be made anywhere, is invisible,
> And does not smell.
>
> (*N* 15)

The capital letters are now attached to the true divinity; "Common Prayer" introduces a worshipful stance and ritual note as the poem reveals itself to be a "rite of homage." It undermines its own spiritual significance: poets are self-centered, solipsistic beings, who deny, reject, and ignore innocent nature for the sake of their own little pleasures. Poetry is not evil; it is just the grown-up version of the teasing playfulness that gets Mommy's attention, the "incorrigible staginess" acknowledged by Auden's Caliban.

"In Praise of Limestone" turns almost literally into a rite as it invokes the Apostles' Creed: "if Sins can be forgiven, if bodies rise from the dead" and "the life to come" echo "I believe in . . . The Forgiveness of sins: The Resurrection of the body: And the Life everlasting." It closes on a note of self-forgetfulness:

> Dear, I know nothing of
> Either, but when I try to imagine a faultless love
> Or the life to come, what I hear is the murmur
> Of underground streams, what I see is a limestone landscape.
> (*N* 16)

In this aetiological narrative the poet defines himself and his art and all art in terms of limestone: poetry is not-limestone, and limestone is not-text, the pure world unsullied by ink, untainted by thought. "In Praise of Limestone" is a poem of *Sehnsucht*, of longing for what is not itself. My own existence, it says, is derivative, and the not-me comprehends all value. I know there is something outside this poem, and I long for it. It is something I am homesick for, and something I "try to imagine": it can only be described by my feelings of longing for it. It is a power I am disturbed, reproached, and loved by.

"In Praise of Limestone" describes its own spiritual failures, but not despairingly. They are acknowledged, accepted, lived with, and even loved. (The more adult version of "displaying his dildo" may be the poet's pleasure in his own naughty and not very significant art.) The mild castigations of limestone, as the poet imagines them, are not a sign of utter and absolute separation from what is spiritually valuable, not a cause for self-flagellation. The poet finds pleasure in imagining a connection with limestone, and in cheerfully, charmingly, winningly writing his good-natured poem. He is still singing "for effects that bring down the house," and in fact Auden did bring down a house of sorts, winning (in this period alone) a Pulitzer Prize in 1948, the Bollingen Prize in 1952, and a National Book Award in 1956. To describe the origin of poetry is both to advertise its triviality and to pay homage to the untrivial substance from which it derives. The tone of apology modulates into the tone of worship.

III

"Memorial for the City" is its own subject: it is the story of art's failed attempts to substitute itself for spiritual value. Literary art in particular studies its own failings here. "Memorial for the City" is "Il Penseroso" to "L'Allegro" of "In Praise of Limestone." It does not pay homage to non-art, the outside-poetry; it denigrates itself, and becomes its own epitaph. The poem is the City whose memorial it describes.

The poem's epigraph and four sections appear to indicate a cyclic movement, moving from the "City of God" referred to in the epigraph through a recital of selected secular events, a kind of "Highlights of Western History: Homer to World War II," to the Flesh anticipating its resurrection. Within this cycle, the general direction of the poem is chronological, with the major periods of Western European history recognizable to a schoolchild: the Crusades, the Reformation, the Renaissance, the French Revolution.

But the order of the sections is subtler and more complex: "Memorial for the City" is composed of increasingly self-conscious rhetorical modes, so that the awareness that art has attempted to substitute itself for spiritual truths emerges only gradually in the poem. The poem is an example of such a failed attempt: what matters is not the "chronological" order the sections delineate but their increasing self-consciousness, as the poem's undermining of its own, earlier arrogation of spiritual authority comes to the surface.

The epigraph forms an important part of this progression, because it begins the poem with a statement claiming to be direct revelation.[12]

> *In the self-same point that our soul is made sensual, in the self-same point is the City of God ordained to him from without beginning.*
>
> *Juliana of Norwich*
> (*N* 39)

[12] Auden probably found this quotation in Charles Williams, *The Descent of the Dove* (1939; New York, 1956), 224.

In its absolute, unselfconscious confidence it resembles the quotation from Emily Brontë that opens *The Sea and the Mirror*. The full title of Dame Julian's work is *Revelations of Divine Love*; her scribe in the postscript writes that "this revelation contains deep theology and great wisdom."[13] The simple declarative prose that is the first thing we read in "Memorial for the City" is literature that sees itself as pure spiritual value, as divinely inspired truth. Dame Julian did not "create" her book; God *revealed* its contents to her. She may undermine herself, her education, and her spiritual worth, but what is in her book is the truth *that has been shown to her*.

Auden's speaker—or one of them—enters the poem in part 1 as a voice of abstract metaphysical statement. This is a voice that lays down the law: this is what Homer's world was like; this is what our world is like, and "We are not to despair." The voice speaks with authority, and evinces no doubt in itself. It refers to "loudspeakers" as if to distinguish them from its own wisdom, but in fact this person is something of an orator. He announces definitively what "Homer's world" was like: "gods behave, men die, / Both feel in their own small way," but the earth "Does nothing and does not care, / She alone is seriously there."[14] But, says the confident speaker, this view is *wrong*, or at least it is no longer valid: "Our grief is not Greek." In the lines that end this section Auden adopts "the preacher's loose, immodest tone." His utterances sound as if they were delivered from the pulpit:

> We know without knowing there is reason for what we bear,
> That our hurt is not a desertion, that we are to pity
> Neither ourselves nor our city;

[13] Julian of Norwich, *Revelations of Divine Love*, ed. and trans. Clifton Wolters (Harmondsworth and Baltimore, 1966), 213.

[14] Auden's examples of "Homer's world" and his term "Post-Virgilian City" are based on the distinctions between "Primary Epic" and "Secondary Epic" made by C. S. Lewis in *A Preface to Paradise Lost* (Oxford, 1942; repr. 1961), 29–30, 37–39. They are not adequately explained by the passage in *The Descent of the Dove* to which Fuller refers readers (*Reader's Guide*, 226).

Whoever the searchlights catch,
　　　　　　　　　　whatever the loudspeakers blare,
We are not to despair.

(*N* 40)

Why not? Who is this "we," and how does the speaker of "Memorial for the City" know the ultimate truths of the universe?

Auden does not, like Dame Julian, claim a divine authority for what he propounds. This is not revelation, just theological assertion. And whether the assertions are about "life" or about literature is not altogether clear: "Homer's" world is a fictive one, not necessarily to be identified with any actual period in Greek civilization. And if we now live "Among the ruins of the Post-Vergilian City," does that mean that "we" live in an epic? The speaker of this section is only slightly more self-conscious than Dame Julian; he does not purport to be uttering revealed truth. His oracular pronouncements claim authority yet naively blur theology and literary criticism.

In the first section of "Memorial for the City," then, the poem does not undermine its own spiritual significance: it speaks in a language confident of its authority. Its subject appears to be ultimate religious truths, which it utters solemnly and unselfconsciously. In the second section of the poem, the form abruptly becomes more artificial: the internal rhyming increases dramatically, and a strict stanzaic form, seven lines alternately indented, takes over from the loose verse paragraphs of the opening section.[15] The form, that is, becomes more self-conscious of itself *as a form* rather than simply a series of statements with occasionally rhyming words. The subject of this section is not ultimate religious truths, but art's—and particularly literature's—conscious attempts to

[15] As Fuller points out (*Reader's Guide*, 226), Auden's mode of internal rhyming here (and also in "In Praise of Limestone") comes via Charles Williams. But as Auden appropriates this rhyming he makes it his own, using it with increasing intensity to mark art's substitution of itself for religious truths.

substitute itself for ultimate religious truths.[16] Its narrative line tells a story of secularization, as Pope and Emperor struggle for dominance and religious ideas are used to justify political actions like the Crusades. The scholastic philosophers, who "fought to recover thought / From the eccentricities of the private brain," turned spiritual truths into philosophic argument. Benignly, prettily, spiritual concepts became embodied in stained glass:

> . . . framed in her windows, orchards, ports,
> Wild beasts, deep rivers and dry rocks
> Lay nursed on the smile of a merciful Madonna.
>
> (*N* 41)

After Luther, there is a bursting out of secular, artistic energies. This period is of course commonly known as the Renaissance, but Auden is not interested in historians' labels. His concern lies in what art thinks it can do:

> Saints tamed, poets acclaimed the raging herod of the will;
> The groundlings wept as on a secular stage
> The grand and the bad went to ruin in thundering verse;
> Sundered by reason and treason the City
> Found invisible ground for concord in measured sound,
> While wood and stone learned the shameless
> Games of man, to flatter, to show off, be pompous, to romp.
>
> (*N* 41)

Art takes for its subject spiritual struggles: the "raging herod" is the figure of the mystery plays and his descendants, grand and bad heroes like Faustus and Macbeth. Ecclesiastic music and hymns take on a spiritual responsibility: the Protestant reformers, as Auden says elsewhere, "had to replace the Catholic expressions of unity which they had destroyed with a new

[16] In all of "Memorial for the City" and in this section particularly Auden subverts for his own purposes the storyline of *The Descent of the Dove* and Williams's emphasis on the role of the Holy Spirit in the history of the Church.

one, namely music."[17] Baroque sculpture and architecture continue the process begun by stained glass, only now (this is Auden's interpretation, in the poem and in an essay of the same period) instead of expressing a truth outside itself, "religious" art expresses itself as spiritually significant: the "architect is no longer the midwife who brings forth from matter its latent soul but the potter whose will imposes on a neutral substance whatever shape he fancies."[18] The natural materials, wood and stone, are being "exploited for religious purposes."

In the rollicking internal rhyme of "the shameless Games of man" and "to show off, be pompous, to romp," the second part of "Memorial for the City" is itself romping, and the poem embodies the kind of flaunting it describes, flaunting all the more when it talks about flaunting. This is a clue to the fact that parts, at least, of "Memorial for the City" have the same aspirations to spiritual significance as the very art Auden is describing. See, for instance, the final two stanzas of the second section, which treat mockingly the romantic poets' "hectic quest for the prelapsarian man," their quest for something spiritually valuable away from the secular wasteland of ordinary society:

> The deserts were dangerous, the waters rough, their clothes
> 	Absurd but, changing their Beatrices often,
> Sleeping little, they pushed on, raised the flag of the Word
> 	Upon lawless spots denied or forgotten
> By the fear or the pride of the Glittering City;
> 	Guided by hated parental shades,
> They invaded and harrowed the hell of her natural self.
>
> Chimeras mauled them, they wasted away with the spleen,
> 	Suicide picked them off; sunk off Cape Consumption,
> Lost on the Tosspot Seas, wrecked on the Gibbering Isles
> 	Or trapped in the ice of despair at the Soul's Pole,

[17] Auden, introduction to *Elizabethan and Jacobean Poets* (New York, 1950), xxiii.

[18] Auden, introduction to *Elizabethan and Jacobean Poets*, xxii.

They died, unfinished, alone; but now the forbidden,
The hidden, the wild outside were known:
Faithful without faith, they died for the Conscious City.
(*N* 42)

In these inspired stanzas Auden deprecates the romantics for treating the events of their lives and their created works as spiritually significant. If they are "changing their Beatrices often," they have a pretty silly idea of Beatrice, because there is only *one* Beatrice: they are Dante manqué. The "Word" they preach, with capital letter, is their own *logos*. "Faithful without faith," they are faithful to their solitary quests on behalf of imaginative and literary value, but without conventional religious "faith" in a deity worshipped by other people (like Brontë in "Plead for me").

The romantics form part of a tradition of artists who (in Auden's view) take upon themselves the authority to utter spiritual truths. They close the second section of "Memorial for the City" because Auden sees the period from the late Middle Ages through the nineteenth century in an almost Spenglerian way as the exhaustion of the secularizing impulse of several hundred years. The apocalyptic vision of "Memorial for the City" is not all that far from that of *The Dance of Death*, in which Karl Marx appears at the finale to announce the death of the exhausted bourgeois Dancer. The history of Europe from the eleventh century through the nineteenth is the story of art's gradual arrogation to itself of the spiritual authority of the Church. That does not mean that it actually gets that authority, but that it talks (and sculpts, and composes) as if it did.

But there is an important contradiction here that the poem does not seem aware of: why can *some* poetry speak with spiritual authority? The joke about Beatrice implies that Dante's poetry is valid and the romantics' is not. Beatrice was Dante's fictional creation: a poet may of course have in mind an actual breathing human being when he or she creates a character, but, for such an idealized one particularly, why *not* see aspects of the ideal in any number of actual women? Is that any sillier than seeing those aspects in one? And if the romantics secularize and taint with their poetic "Word" any pure innocent "spot" they find, is not Auden doing the same thing in this poem? If they cannot write about matters of ultimate spiritual value in their poetry, how can any poet?

Auden would have to answer something like what Eliot said about Yeats's *A Vision* in *After Strange Gods*, namely, that Yeats's supernatural world was the "wrong supernatural world."[19] Auden's mockery of the romantic poets in these stanzas assumes that his supernatural world is right and theirs are not. The lines about suicide and consumption are slightly hyperbolic: Blake and Wordsworth both lived to be seventy. (Auden himself died at sixty-six, but of course he could not have predicted that at the age of forty-one, when he wrote "Memorial for the City.")

The second section of "Memorial for the City" is conscious, then, of art's attempt to substitute itself for scripture, but does not see that issue as relevant to itself. If someone says "Our hurt is not a desertion," is he not purporting to speak for "the Word"? Does not that theological point then become his or her poetic "words" rather than religious doctrine? Preachy as he may sound, the speaker of "Memorial for the City" is not in a pulpit. Auden in his prose would have agreed: "I sometimes wonder if there is not something a bit questionable, from a Christian point of view, about all works of art which make overt Christian references. They seem to assert that there is such a thing as a Christian culture, which there cannot be. Culture is one of Caesar's things. . . . The only kind of literature which has gospel authority is the parable" (*DH* 458).

The barbed wire in the third section divides culture from ultimate spiritual value. It is yet another version of the uncrossable border in Auden's earliest poems, the border that divides the frozen place from the orchard, the isolated from the community, the spy from his fellows, and lovers from each

[19] T. S. Eliot, *After Strange Gods: A Primer of Modern Heresy* (London, 1934), 46.

other. The barbed wire "erases" the pattern and design of the City: all attempts to create value will always come up against it. This section of "Memorial for the City" takes for granted that the "City" built by culture for itself is "burnt-out," "damaged," "abolished." The third section does not attempt to make any religious statements: it does not arrogate spiritual authority to itself, as part 2 did, by making fun of artists who wrongly arrogate spiritual authority to themselves.

What is this value on the other side, this something that culture, Caesar's thing, can never reach? Does it not have to be like those "lawless spots denied or forgotten" that the romantics sought out, an entity that cannot possibly be described in the poet's words without ceasing to be the Word? That would be true if Auden proceeded to speak *ex cathedra*, but he does not: he speaks *ex sceana*. Part 3 gradually becomes theatrical and introduces a dramatic character. Auden changes from preacher to presenter: when he says that the wire and ruins are not the end for the "Image," he is not purporting to utter ultimate truth but to describe a dramatic character:

> Behind the wire
> Which is behind the mirror, our Image is the same
> Awake or dreaming . . .
>
> Is It our friend?
> No; that is our hope; that we weep and It does not grieve,
> That for It the wire and the ruins are not the end:
> This is the flesh we are but never would believe,
> The flesh we die but it is death to pity;
> This is Adam waiting for His City.
>
> *Let Our Weakness speak.*
>
> (*N* 43)

The italicized final sentence marks the stage border between presenter and character, outer and inner play. The barbed wire and the slow revelation of "It" suggests that this being will resemble the Man-Woman who spoke from behind barbed wire in John Nower's dream, the erotic value that, if transformed, could redeem a whole society.

The spirit is willing but the flesh is weak, we know, and Auden says this is "Our Weakness." Philosophically, this flesh is the same entity as the rock and water of limestone, all those innocent athletes, the nude young man displaying his dildo: this is innocent creatureliness, fresh from Genesis, uncontaminated by the will. But that would be in another poem. "Memorial for the City" demonstrates its newfound wisdom by making the purest and most innocent being speak in the most theatrical and artificial way. This is not Adam waiting for His City; this is Caliban reborn, the flesh showing its awareness of grace by renouncing its own importance. Caliban initially differentiates himself from the previous sections of *The Sea and the Mirror* by implying he is on the near side of the curtain, outside the play, and only gradually speaks of his "incorrigible staginess." Here the whole poem enacts a gradual coming to consciousness of staginess, and the final stage of that awareness is evident in the theatrical presentation of a character who defines himself as not-culture. Here is the final wisdom of the poem: that its final section not only does not attempt to sound like scripture; it "flaunts" its artifice.

And so "Our Weakness" is flippant, playful, arrogant, claiming personal involvement in the high points of Western literature and myth and taking personal credit for the more notorious events therein:

> Without me Adam would have fallen irrevocably with Lucifer;
> he would have never have been able to cry *O felix culpa*.
> It was I who suggested his theft to Prometheus; my frailty cost
> Adonis his life.
>
> (*N* 43)

This is no modest, unselfconscious body, but a stagy presence who is very pleased with himself and enjoys thoroughly the role he is playing. Like baroque architecture, he is showing off, being pompous, romping. He makes no statements whatsoever about God, or the significance of suffering or despair, or the superiority of Christianity to romanticism. His monologue is a charming capsule summary of "The Role of the

Flesh in Literature and Myth." In the story he tells, all the grand and the bad were less clever than he: Oedipus, Faustus, Hamlet, Don Quixote, the Ancient Mariner, Ahab, approached wisdom only to the extent that they acknowledged the superior value of the flesh. Here is his finale:

> As for Metropolis, that too-great city; her delusions are not
> mine.
> Her speeches impress me little, her statistics less; to all who dwell
> on the public side of her mirrors resentments and no peace.
> At the place of my passion her photographers are gathered
> together; but I shall rise again to hear her judged.
>
> (*N* 44)

The flesh sees himself *sub specie culturae*, as an aspect of Culture, of Caesar's things. He is on public display, a subject for photography.[20] Although what he says is theologically consistent with what Dame Julian saw in her "shewings," from a literary point of view it is entirely different. This flesh views everything as a matter of speeches: he himself is a stage character making a very rhetorical speech, a veritable litany of sentences. Metropolis makes speeches; and all he knows of the City of God is an anticipated speech, the verbal aspect of the Last Judgment: "I shall rise again to hear her judged." And notice that he carefully says of Metropolis, "her delusions are not mine": he does not say that he has no delusions, only that his are different.

"Memorial for the City" does then finally announce the demise of the city and become its own epitaph, as its final character imagines the condemnation of the city at the end of time. A poem that is one of the city's own artifacts condemns the city already; who needs to wait for the Last Judgment? The city has already been judged. And since such a stagy theatrical

[20] Compare Auden's comments in 1948 on stereotypical "contemporary" attitudes to the Crucifixion: that it was "actually performed" by the French; that the "English said, 'Oh, dear!' and consented" and the Americans "said, 'How undemocratic!' and sent photographers" (*FA* 14).

poem can only be—as it finally realizes—one more "secular stage," one more speech, the poem renounces its own importance as it denies culture spiritual value. The real flesh, if such a personification could be imagined outside of literature, could not speak, and certainly would not be wittily alluding to Orpheus, Plato, Arthurian romance, Hamlet, and Don Giovanni. As Auden had already written, silence is ripeness and ripeness all. This clever being is a performer wearing a flesh-costume.

IV

Horae Canonicae takes a comprehensive view of poetry, and art generally, as trivial and insignificant by placing it in the context of civic life. This is not, like "Memorial for the City," a diachronic perspective on art's attempts through the ages to substitute itself for spiritual value, nor does the series of seven poems develop in awareness of its own implication in art's triviality. Nor, like "Shield of Achilles," does *Horae Canonicae* work by *praeteritio*, specifying the compassion and love it cannot talk about. Poetry is undermined yet ultimately accepted in *Horae Canonicae* because it is part of the texture of ordinary life. Poetry is seen neither as a fraudulent spirituality nor as a disappointment of its audience's expectations: it is seen as one of many vocations, the artifact produced by one of numerous activities occurring daily in the city.

That *Horae Canonicae* should derive its structure from the chiming of bells at regular intervals suggests the necessary accommodation of poetry and all other activities to what is. The canonical hours are not, of course, Auden's invention. Their origin in the life of the monastic community, in ancient religious tradition, and their more fundamental association with the sun's passage across the sky—all of these connections show the subordination of imagination to the facts of the external world. Like bees and ants (see "Vespers"), poets and surgeons live within the confines of natural fact and communal life. Much has been written about the religious background of *Horae Canonicae*, but it is significant, I think, that the series wears its religion lightly.[21] It does not talk directly about Christ or the Crucifixion; it avoids proper names. As a series *Horae Canonicae* accepts poetry's limitations and confines its subject to the secular implications of religious ideas.

Horae Canonicae is not "about" the insignificance of poetry. Poetry is one part of a larger civic life whose guilt is assessed in the series. The poet does not enter until the second poem, "Terce." In a way his importance is undermined because he is not treated with any fanfare (I am using the masculine pronoun because Auden does in the series). The self that awakens in "Prime," with its will that chooses, its arm that acts, its memory that praises and blames and conveniently forgets—this self is differentiated vocationally, throughout the series, into the population of a whole city. In "Terce" the poet is introduced as the last of a triad: the hangman who "does not know yet who will be provided / To do the high works of justice with," the judge who "does not know by what sentence / He will apply on earth the Law that rules the stars," and the poet who,

taking a breather
Round his garden before starting his eclogue,
Does not know whose Truth he will tell.

(*SA* 65)

[21] The best book on the religious background of *Horae Canonicae* has nothing to do with Auden. It is A.-M. Roguet, O.P., *The Liturgy of the Hours: The General Instruction with Commentary*, trans. Peter Coughlan and Peter Purdue (Collegeville, Minnesota, 1971). See, for instance, the final chapter, "The Liturgy of the Hours in Our Lives": "Our *daily work*, even housework or work in a factory, is linked with the Liturgy of the Hours in a double way. First of all because it is a *cosmic* liturgy, especially by reason of the psalms, which lend a voice of praise to the whole of material creation—'the earth and all its fullness'—and to the world of nature which work perfects and transforms. It is a liturgy of Hours: arranged over the different periods of our day, it gives significance to our *entire* life by throwing its light on all the moments and occupations of our *daily* life. This is particularly evident in the 'Prayers' at Lauds which consecrate the efforts of the day which is about to begin; in the Middle Hour which is above all concerned with sanctifying work in the middle of the day; in Compline, which closes the day with an expression of trust" (140).

The poet's spiritual significance is undermined in a number of ways already here. The company in which he is introduced is thoroughly secular: the first is someone who kills people for the state, the second someone who condemns people to die. They are characterized as bureaucratic functionaries, and their impersonality rubs off on the poet: he, too, is seen as a functionary, coolly preparing to write an automatic poem about someone or other. The attitude to the poet is reductive: he is neither more nor less important than the other two. He is one of a group. And in addition, the context implies that maybe there ought to be some spiritual concern here on the part of these three detached, complicit citizens.

Any elevated notion of the poet's function in society—that, for instance, he reminds the society of values that it might otherwise forget, that he inspires sympathy and compassion, that he teaches people to unlearn hatred and learn love—any such notion is undermined when the poet is presented in a series in such a way that he might as well be the undertaker.

"Sext" further secularizes the poet by insistently placing him among more and more miscellaneous workers, surgeons, clerks, flint-flakers, and cooks. As a "mouth," the poet is linked with the judicial mouths that mete out death sentences. "You may not like them much," Auden writes,

> . . . but we owe them
>
> basilicas, divas,
> dictionaries, pastoral verse,
>
> the courtesies of the city:
> without these judicial mouths . . .
>
> how squalid existence would be,
> tethered for life to some hut village,
>
> afraid of the local snake
> or the local ford demon,
>
> speaking the local patois
> of some three hundred words. . . .
>
> (*SA* 69)

Joined with grand opera and capital punishment, poetry is both luxury entertainment and guilty civic function. Either way, its virtues, such as they are, have nothing spiritual about them. By its triviality or by its moral callousness, poetry is implicated in the victim's death. Pastoral verse is of course a "courtesy of the city" because it is poetry of longing for rural life written by urban poets. But poets have no more spiritual powers than others in the poem's lists, cooks or collectors of seashells. Poetry is one of the comforts of civilization that make life less "squalid," like indoor plumbing. To think of it in terms of something truly important in any ultimate sense would be out of the question.

"Vespers" more forcefully condemns all art as complicit in society's guilt. The Arcadian, ostentatiously trivial and amoral, almost proudly reveals a personality in which fastidiousness and artistic sensibility dominate. Conspicuously avoiding compassion and sympathy, he looks the other way "Passing a slum child with rickets." An aesthete who likes Bellini, medieval music, and Romanesque architecture, he does not associate any of his tastes with any other kind of value than the beautiful. By seeing his earnest radical counterpart, the Utopian, he is forced, he says, "to remember our victim," to have something spiritually significant brought home to him. For one moment in the twenty-four hours, he understands his distance from value, and his complicity in the victim's death.

In "Compline" the poet makes a last, guilty appearance. He now longs to come in contact with some ultimate religious truth, but such contact would occur in spite of, not because of, his poetry:

> Can poets (can men in television)
> Be saved? It is not easy
> To believe in unknowable justice. . . .
>
> (*SA* 82)

The poet's vocation is once more juxtaposed to a job that is not on the spiritual map, one so insignificant that poetry is denigrated merely by the proximity. Poets are among the final secular figures mentioned in *Horae Canonicae* because their spiritual fate is of some concern to Auden, and it is his hope that—in spite of their guilt, their silliness, their insignificance—they may come in touch with value.

Unlike "In Praise of Limestone," *Horae Canonicae* does not see poets as narcissistically pleased with themselves. Unlike "Memorial for the City," it does not see them as arrogantly attempting to take over religious functions. Quite simply, it sees poets as like everyone else, no better and no worse than judges, hangmen, or men in television. As citizens they are as responsible for society's victims as anyone else, as complicit in their deaths, and as necessary to the ordinary functioning of the city. Poets and poetry are not important, but they are not less important than the ordinary run of human activities.

What, then, is "Lauds" doing at the end of this series? What does it mean to have a highly artificial poem, about God and neighborly love and a happy productive community, in the simple and idealized language of a nursery rhyme, after poetry has been so definitively separated from spiritual value? Auden has already bowed offstage with the final reference to poets in "Compline," much as he bows out of "In Praise of Limestone" (the poet who calls his mind Puzzle) and, later, "Homage to Clio" (why should Clio read the poets). Here, *after* his deferential, self-deprecatory gesture, is another poem.

The presence of "Lauds" implies that the poet is still functioning. He is beginning another day, bright and early. His acknowledgment of guilt has not precluded his activity as a poet. It is time to begin again, and understanding of guilt need not lead to paralysis. There is something liberating about having admitted and acknowledged the uselessness and frivolity of his art. In "Lauds" Auden is being deliberately artificial, flaunting his skill. If *Horae Canonicae* were a meal he would have ended with something flambé: "Lauds" has that same showy, virtuoso quality about it. With its intricate interweaving of Nature and History, it is a miniature *Horae Canonicae*.[22] Having confessed his sins, the poet, with all his spiritu-

[22] The odd-numbered tercets begin with iambs and descriptions of "natu-

ally insignificant skills, is now free to play, and he does. The poem asks for God's blessing on all secular activities: "God bless the Realm, God bless the People; / God bless this green world temporal."

The innocence of "Lauds" is *faux-naïf*: where now is the victim? Where are injustice, exploitation, suffering, guilt, indifference, all the evils of the city? The poet has not forgotten them; he ends with a highly artful, artificial piece because it is pretty, because it is a new day, because his imagination is energetic, and because that is what it is his vocation to do. The acknowledgment of guilt did not mean that he was going to *stop* writing poetry. His guilt is original sin; he cannot avoid it. But the release that comes with confession and with imagining himself saved, as he does in the final lines of "Compline," inspires the elegant, pretty poem he closes with, an offering to the new day.

V

In one of the most moving examples of Auden's *veneratio poetarum*, "The Cave of Making," all the spiritual awareness Auden denies himself is attributed to Louis MacNeice. In a mode that began with *New Year Letter* and continued in "In Praise of Limestone" and "Homage to Clio," Auden here praises a remote, idealized figure and apologizes for himself.

MacNeice is seen as a fellow poet and kindred spirit, "with whom I / once collaborated, once at a weird Symposium / exchanged winks as a juggins / went on about Alienation." Clearly, Auden is not alienated if he has got someone to exchange winks with. Somehow MacNeice, through death, has been washed clean of all the triviality and guilt associated with poetry. Like the great Masters invoked in *New Year Letter*, or like Henry James in the poem at his grave, MacNeice is treated as a moral and spiritual superior, a "voice of conscience." Au-

ral" phenomena; the even-numbered begin with trochees and descriptions of events that are, in Auden's specialized use of the term, "historical."

den ends the main part of the elegy with what is virtually a prayer to St. Louis:

Seeing you know our mystery
from the inside and therefore
how much, in our lonely dens, we need the companionship
of our good dead, to give us
comfort on dowly days when the self is a nonentity
dumped on a mound of nothing,
to break the spell of our self-enchantment when lip-smacking
imps of mawk and hooey
write with us what they will, you won't think me imposing if
I ask you to stay at my elbow
until cocktail time: dear Shade, for your elegy
I should have been able to manage
something more like you than this egocentric monologue,
but accept it for friendship's sake.

(*AH* 11)

MacNeice is invoked to save Auden from the kind of imps he described in "Cattivo Tempo," the anti-muse that makes him write "self-enchanted" poetry. Presumably MacNeice was not there soon enough, because the poem goes out condemning itself as an "egocentric monologue." (Here Auden is the poet who calls his mind Puzzle.) The poem renounces its own spiritual value, condemns itself, and expresses reverence for MacNeice, who (one can infer) is *not* egocentric. MacNeice as voice of conscience is there "until cocktail time" (some few hours beyond this poem, when Auden will perhaps write a less egocentric poem) to keep Auden in line spiritually.

As originally printed in *About the House*, the elegy for MacNeice had a "Postscript" that even more definitively renounced the spiritual significance of Auden's own writing. The final section is worth quoting in full:

Time has taught you
how much inspiration
your vices brought you,
what imagination

can owe temptation
　　　　　　yielded to,
that many a fine
　　　　　　expressive line
would not have existed,
　　　　　　had you resisted:
as a poet, you
　　　　　　know this is true,
and though in Kirk
　　　　　　you sometimes pray
to feel contrite,
　　　　　　it doesn't work.
Felix Culpa, you say:
　　　　　　perhaps you're right.

You hope, yes,
　　　　　　your books will excuse you,
save you from hell:
　　　　　　nevertheless,
without looking sad,
　　　　　　without in any way
seeming to blame
　　　　　　(He doesn't need to,
knowing well
　　　　　　what a lover of art
like yourself pays heed to),
　　　　　　God may reduce you
on Judgment Day
　　　　　　to tears of shame,
reciting by heart,
　　　　　　the poems you would
have written, had
　　　　　　your life been good.

(*AH* 12–13)

Here Auden treats himself as tumbler Barnaby and announces that he considers his faults fortunate ("*Felix Culpa*") because they generate so much poetry. Naughty, naughty me, says the poet, displaying his dildo, pompously romping, being clever, immoral, cheerfully trivial.

But then—because perhaps the Shade MacNeice has not been able to exert much moral suasion over the surviving poet (writing the rest of this, maybe, "until cocktail time"), the sterner figure of God enters in. (As in *New Year Letter*, there are different degrees of moral authority.) *Agenbit of inwit*: it occurs to the poem's speaker that maybe there *does* exist a kind of poetry that, if not spiritually valuable itself, at least emanates from a poet whose life has been good, as Barnaby's tumbling changed its mode from staginess to homage. Auden here undermines not only his own poetry but his life, apologizing for both. In its uncertain confessional mode this poem is like Donne's "Hymn to God the Father": the poet has so much fun confessing to God how naughty he is that it is difficult to know how to read the final act of concession. As the poem of someone with acknowledged "vices," who says he "sometimes" prays to be contrite but "it doesn't work," this cute poem could not itself be an act of contrition. That, presumably, lies in the future, off the page, outside the poetry that is self-condemned.

Caliban grows flabby. The softening of the muscle begins at the end of *Horae Canonicae*, when Auden asks, "Can poets (can men in television) / Be saved?" and soon slips into the colloquialism "all poor s-o-b's who never / Do anything properly." The tense rhythms of Caliban's clauses,

> our shame, our fear, our incorrigible staginess, all wish and no resolve, are still, and more intensely than ever, all we have: only now it is not in spite of them but with them that we are blessed by that Wholly Other Life, (*CP* 402)

the excitement of the epiphanous moment, the profound acceptance of guilt and intuition of blessing—all these are gone, or mutated into softer versions of themselves.

"Narcissus is an oldie," Auden remarks in "Lullaby," one of his last poems, happily, sloppily, self-indulgent:

. . . now you fondle
your almost feminine flesh
with mettled satisfaction,
imagining that you are
sinless and all-sufficient,
snug in the den of yourself. . . .

(*TYF* 39)

Comfy and pleased with his imperfections, Auden loves the very qualities he used to undermine. This is not just an "oldie" displaying his dildo like the boy of "In Praise of Limestone": there every sensual experience was perceived as a gift of limestone, and limestone, as the boy grew separate from it, manifested itself as holy, forgiving, Love. As "*Madonna* and *Bambino*" himself, Auden does not need Elizabeth Mayer or Clio (or limestone, for that matter) to bless him; he is "all-sufficient."

Less often rites of homage to remote deities, or wry, self-deprecating apologies, deferring to *l'hors-texte*, the poems of later Auden tend to be "all-sufficient." "Doggerel by a Senior Citizen" may be less than memorable poetry, but it is typical of the later, baggy-pants Auden. The poet who in "Memorial for the City" revealed the tendency of culture to arrogate spiritual value to itself claims significance for an Anglican-Edwardian bourgeois professional world:

The Book of Common Prayer we knew
Was that of 1662 . . .

Then Speech was mannerly, an Art,
Like learning not to belch or fart . . .

Saner those class-rooms which I sat in,
Compelled to study Greek and Latin.

(*EG* 35)

This fuddy-duddy needs to be "cut short by a sharp voice" like the first speaker of "City without Walls," but he is not.

Horae Canonicae demonstrated that forgiveness may be as dependably recurrent as sin, and the loss of anxiety spells death to Auden's poetry. Auden at the end of his life sounds like the Arcadian of "Vespers," smugly pleased with the refinements of his own civilization, and not too preoccupied by ethical or spiritual matters except "for a fraction of a second." Snug in his own eccentricities, Caliban fondles himself to sleep, undisturbed by his separateness from the Wholly Other Life.

Writing This for You to Open When I Am Gone

For no one goes
Further than railhead or the ends of piers,
Will neither go nor send his son
Further through foothills than the rotting stack
Where gaitered gamekeeper with dog and gun
Will shout "Turn back."
—"Who will endure . . . ," 1930

ALL ACCESS is blocked; the border is absolute. The stage dissolves only to reveal another stage: there is no crossing over. The prompter who echoes Ariel is only a "Prompter"—not a breathing human being like you, outside *The Sea and the Mirror*, but eight black letters on a white page. Poetry makes nothing happen: "if not a poem had been written, not a picture painted, not a bar of music composed, the history of man would be materially unchanged."[1] There is still "no change of place," as Auden wrote in 1930, but the border is now the margin at the side of the page.

Auden's definition of the edge of things shifted from the geographic to the aesthetic in the late 1930s and early 1940s, around the time of his immigration to the United States. In subsequent poems such as the Yeats elegy, *New Year Letter*, *For the Time Being*, *The Sea and the Mirror*, "In Praise of Limestone" and "Memorial for the City," Auden dramatized the barrier or "essential emphatic gulf" (as he termed it in *The Sea and the Mirror*) between poetry and the source of value outside it. His poems began to point out their contingent

[1] Auden, "The Public v. the Late Mr. William Butler Yeats," *Partisan Review* 6, no. 3 (Spring 1939): 51.

status as works of art, and to deny their power to make grand definitive statements about anything except their own insignificance and their author's unworthiness. Rereading literary history and turning it into aesthetic stipulation, Auden's prose argued for a systematic disestablishing of the poet: "We live in a new age in which the artist neither can have such a unique heroic importance nor believes in the Art-God enough to desire it" (*EF* 150). Like *The Enchafèd Flood*, whose peroration begins with the words just quoted, Auden's poems in the years following 1939 require of the poet an act of concession, as he humbles himself before some value he can only know by its absence. The "heroic image," according to *The Enchafèd Flood*, is not the artist "but the less exciting figure of the builder, who renews the ruined walls of the city" (*EF* 150). Subordinating his ego and his creative genius to a communal effort, the artist becomes simply a citizen.

Auden, of course, did not become simply a citizen, but a poet who advertised his profession's unheroic status. Certainly it is appropriate to see this disempowering of poetry as a reaction to romanticism, as many students of Auden have over the years, and as Auden's own literary criticism encourages us to. *The Enchafèd Flood* concerns itself explicitly with the "romantic spirit," and Auden's famous rejections of Shelley's poetics (" 'The unacknowledged legislators of the world' describes the secret police, not the poets" [*DH* 27]) and Yeats's *A Vision* ("Southern Californian") make a frontal attack.[2] Auden's subtlest attack on romanticism's ordination of the poet, and on the attribution of ultimate spiritual good to the imagination, occurs in his use of the Emily Brontë quotation as epigraph to *The Sea and the Mirror*—subtlest, because epigraphs are generally used respectfully, and here the subsequent poem's implicit answer to Brontë's "And am I wrong . . . ?" is Yes. Yes, you are wrong to worship a "God of Visions" created by the self, dwelling in poetry.[3]

[2] Auden, "Yeats as an Example," *Kenyon Review* 10, no. 2 (Spring 1948): 188.

[3] See chapter 3 of this book for a discussion of the Brontë epigraph.

The God of Visions is indeed anathema: ultimate value (this is Auden's reading of the romantics) does not reside in the imagination. Auden's "loudest" poetics reacts primarily to the positions of writers like Brontë and Shelley. But there is another "silent" commentary that forms part of Auden's poetics, a cluster of ideas stronger for being less polemical and less dogmatic. This hidden poetics inheres in Auden's creative revisions of medieval and Renaissance genres and topoi, in his imagination's consistent reaction to what it finds alien. Its emphasis is less a disempowering of literature than a disassociating of it from a responsive audience. Where earlier English literature sees friendly connections, an easy access of the poetic to the extrapoetic, Auden in his rewritings omits connections or denies access.

"Give me your hands if we be friends," announces Puck in a winningly open gesture, asking to shake hands across an ontological boundary as well as requesting applause. "If I were a woman, I would kiss as many of you as had beards that pleased me," remarks Rosalind, implying that the sexual boundary, not the ontological one, prevents her. Dramatis personae and members of the audience can, just possibly, shake hands or kiss because they are all human beings. Auden draws on the medieval and Renaissance traditions of epilogue and prologue, presenter and *plaudite*, only to deny such intercourse. Where Shakespeare returns "home" from the temporary artifice of the play, letting the actor meet the audience halfway to its unartificial world, Auden denies the reality of any such "home." In *For the Time Being* Narrator and audience are joined, if at all, only in their common failure to love and in their "insignificance." The Narrator does not suggest shaking hands or kissing; with dry resignation he associates the deconstructable nature of art's tinsel and broken ornaments with "life's" dirty kitchen tables and broken machines.

So, also, the "Stage Manager to the Critics" and the so-called Prompter's so-called echo in *The Sea and the Mirror* only point inward to the poem's separation from extratextual critics and prompters. Caliban's talk "to the audience" is a soliloquy on the printed page of a closet drama, a talk that closes envisioning the theater as a place of "contrived fissures." A manuscript draft of Caliban's speech shows Auden using something more closely resembling a traditional *plaudite* to deny explicitly the kinds of connections implied in a typical Shakespearean *plaudite*:

> Ladies and gentlemen, please keep your seats.
> An unidentified plane is reported
> Approaching the city. Probably only a false alarm
> But naturally, we cannot afford
> To take any chances. So all our lights are out
> And we must sit in the dark. I can guess
> What you are thinking: How odd this feels: to be sitting
> In a theatre when the final curtain has fallen
> On a dream that ended agreeably with wedding bells
> Substantial rewards for the good, and for the bad
> Nothing worse than a ducking. . . .[4]

This address to the audience states rather baldly the barrier between the work of art and the life on the other side of the "final curtain." Of course the "unidentified plane" and the speech itself are part of the play, so that the extradramatic world is incorporated into the drama, and the border between the two simply pushed farther off. Shakespeare would not make such incursions into the audience's territory, fictionalizing a realm patently beyond the bounds of his play. His tendency is to distance the play itself, apologizing ("If we shadows have offended") or emphasizing the actor's identity as actor (Rosalind, Prospero) or revealing the artifice that gave the character his identity (Rosalind, Feste). The manuscript speech could not really show what art cannot contain (as, for instance, "The Shield of Achilles" does) because whatever the actor says becomes script. And, as Auden no doubt realized, an "unidentified plane" would one day become anachronistic as an instance of the life outside the theater. Certainly the final, published version of Caliban's speech is far subtler,

[4] As transcribed in Spears, *Poetry of W. H. Auden*, 249.

but the manuscript reveals Auden's obsession with the eternal separation between the work of art and the audience.

When Auden (and Chester Kallman) rewrote George Peele's *Old Wives Tale* as *Delia: or A Masque of Night*, they omitted one of the chief charms of the original play, the figures that mediate between the play and the audience.[5] In Peele, the three chummy pages Antic, Frolic, and Fantastic constitute an on-stage audience, and the play is the story told them by the Smith's "old wife" Madge. "A merry winter's tale would drive away the time trimly," remarks Antic, and so the old gammer tells them one:

> Once upon a time, there was a king, or a lord, or a duke, that had a fair daughter, the fairest that ever was . . . and once upon a time his daughter was stolen away. . . . O Lord, I quite forgot! There was a conjurer, and this conjurer could do any thing.[6]

The characters come alive from her tale (as they used to step out of the two-dimensional drawing made by Pat Michaels in the 1950s television show "The Magic Cottage"), act out the play, and "exeunt" when Delia is rescued. Madge wakes up from her snooze and invites the three pages to a homey breakfast of ale and cheese and toast.

The replication of drama and audience on the stage distances the archaic elements of the play and also indicates the easy intercourse between the work of art and the social life it emerges from. *The Old Wives Tale* is paramount among plays of the late 1580s and early 1590s in its "attempt to maintain a sense of contact with the audience . . . and at the same time create a self-contained play."[7] Auden and Kallman's version is a "Libretto for a One-Act Opera," as "literary" and artificial as Peele's play, and as much a reworking of traditional materials, yet its significant omission is the mirroring of a relation-

[5] W. H. Auden and Chester Kallman, *Delia: or A Masque of Night*, *Botteghe Oscure*, 12 (Autumn, 1953): 164–210.

[6] George Peele, *The Old Wives Tale*, in C. F. Tucker Brooke and Nathaniel Burton Paradise, eds., *English Drama 1580–1642* (Boston, 1933), 26.

[7] Mary G. Free, "Audience within Audience in *The Old Wives Tale*," *Renaissance Papers* (1983): 53–61.

ship between art and audience. Auden's own comment on the Elizabethan period is relevant here: "The artist was still sufficiently rooted in the life of his age to feel in common with his audience" (*EA* 364).

A miniature allusion to another Renaissance work occurs within *The Sea and the Mirror* like a tiny framed picture, a little vignette of *The Winter's Tale* at the end of Alonso's "letter" to Ferdinand:

> Blue the sky beyond her humming sail
> As I sit today by our ship's rail
> Watching exuberant porpoises
> Escort us homeward and writing this
> For you to open when I am gone:
> Read it, Ferdinand, with the blessing
> Of Alonso, your father, once King
> Of Naples, now ready to welcome
> Death, but rejoicing in a new love,
> A new peace, having heard the solemn
> Music strike and seen the statue move
> To forgive our illusion.
>
> (*CP* 368–69)

Consider what the scene alluded to is like in *The Winter's Tale*.[8] In the most amazing scene in Shakespeare, art and nature dissolve into one another; as Polixenes has said earlier, "The art itself is nature." The cold stone statue of Hermione becomes "warm life," yet the warm life is an actor dramatizing Shakespeare's art. And yet the skin and lips and veins whose reality Leontes admires are indeed real skin and lips and veins: the actor is a living, breathing human being. Art and nature are a Möbius strip, seemingly different planes yet actually connected without break or division. The statue moves, but the statue was never really a statue, nor the nonstatuesque "real" people.

Auden's allusion cuts off all the connections Shakespeare implies. This moving statue is a metaphor in a letter to be

[8] Act 5, scene 4 of *The Winter's Tale*.

opened when its author is dead. The speaker's claim to a "new love" has been undermined before it is uttered: in the introductory poem of "The Supporting Cast, Sotto Voce" Antonio has already impugned such a claim with his "What a lot a little music can do," so the "solemn music" is of uncertain value as soon as it is mentioned. Prospero himself has referred to the rest of the cast as "extravagant children" who have gotten the punishments they deserve. And all these remarks are made in a poem whose opening has identified ultimate spiritual "ripeness" with the unquotable. The Hermiones in Auden's poetry, Elizabeth Mayer and limestone and Clio, never quite make contact with the naughty men who want their forgiveness and blessing. The Virgin steps out of her niche to bless Barnaby in a poem that is an exercise in an old-fashioned form, demonstrating the blessings available to the innocent and illiterate.

In addition to these revisions of dramatic conventions, Auden revises a topos of lyric poetry, the *retractio*. When a medieval or Renaissance poet wrote a *retractio*, he or she announced a change of poetic mode and tone. Confessing the naughtiness, vanity, and frivolity of her former poetry, the poet acknowledged a need for forgiveness and expressed a resolve to write religious poems in the future, this poem itself, the *retractio*, marking the border between silly and serious poetry.[9] Like an epilogue or prologue, the *retractio* concedes its own reality before a greater one that it confidently addresses.

The assumption—or the fiction—of such poems, as of "The Ballad of Barnaby," is that staginess is corrigible. Thus, for example, Herrick's "His Prayer for Absolution," one of the opening poems of *His Noble Numbers: Or, His Pious Pieces*:

> For Those my unbaptized Rhimes,
> Writ in my wild unhallowed Times;
> For every sentence, clause, and word,
> That's not inlaid with Thee, (my Lord)
> Forgive me, God, and blot each Line

[9] For a complete discussion of the *retractio* as a topos, see Olive Sayce, "Chaucer's 'Retractions': The Conclusion of the *Canterbury Tales* and Its Place in Literary Tradition," *Medium Aevum* 40, no. 3 (1971): 230–48.

Out of my Book, that is not thine.
But if, 'mongst all, Thou find'st here one
Worthy thy Benediction;
That One of all the rest, shall be
The Glory of my Work, and Me.[10]

The mere fact of print and ink is not alienating from God; poetry is not (for Herrick) by nature inauthentic. Such a thing as a "sincere" and "religious" poem exists, a poem expressing some kind of spiritual value. Chaucer's retraction of "many a song and many a leccherous lay" is another famous example of the topos, as is Fulke Greville's poem 84 from *Caelica*, which begins "Farewell sweet boy complain not of my truth" and ends, "But, Cupid, now farewell, I will go play me / With thoughts that please me less, and less betray me."[11]

Like the author of a *retractio*, Auden condemns his own poetry for its vanity and triviality. But he condemns it repeatedly, and repents repeatedly, because Auden sees triviality as the inevitable nature of poetry, a quality built into it. A poem in which the poet promises to write religious poetry hereafter is still a stage on which the poet shows off his artistic skills: Donne is as flirtatious and theatrical in "Hymn to God the Father" as he is in "The Canonization." Herrick (this would be Auden's view) is no closer to any "God" in *His Noble Numbers* than he is to Julia or Anthea in the poems in *Hesperides*: the proper names are all fictions, the poems all secular. Auden writes instead something like a *retractio* manqué, poems that ask for forgiveness but never assume that a spiritually pure poem is a possibility. So in "At the Grave of Henry James," Auden prays to a fellow writer:

All will be judged. Master of nuance and scruple,
Pray for me and for all writers, living or dead;
    Because there are many whose works

[10] *The Poems of Robert Herrick* (Oxford, 1902), 311.

[11] *Selected Poems of Fulke Greville*, ed. with an introduction by Thom Gunn (London, 1968), 117.

Are in better taste than their lives; because there is no end
To the vanity of our calling: make intercession
For the treason of all clerks.

(*CP* 130)

There is "no end" to the vanity of poets, even if they write poems calling attention to their vanity. In the elegy for MacNeice Auden condemns his own poem as an "egocentric monologue," but does not promise to write a more selfless one. The "Postscript" implies that a spiritually better person than Auden might have written better poems, but it does not say they would have been religious poems. The subject matter of the hypothetical poems God "may" recite is never mentioned.

In Auden's reading, *The Tempest* is also a *retractio* manqué, a *retractio* because Prospero gives up magic to think about the more serious matter of death, and because many of the characters abandon vanity and illusion; manqué because, as Auden sees it, they can only become conscious of magic as magic, or illusion as illusion, and not of any final reality. They cannot go any further, philosophically, than an endless iteration of *The Tempest*'s last scene, and that is what Auden writes in *The Sea and the Mirror*. Auden's characters exist "later" than Shakespeare's not in time or in their approach to "truth" but in their awareness of theatricality and illusion. For Auden, there is no such thing as a *retractio* because art is bound by its own inauthentic nature.

And so Auden's closure, his Shantih, is the bringing of the artist to the edge of his art, where he attempts to look out at some spiritual absolute but is able only to look back at the poem itself. At the endings of *New Year Letter*, *The Sea and the Mirror*, "The Cave of Making," Auden pulls back from the Last Judgment to talk about artistic imperfection. Those who judge condemn poetry, and those who bless don't read it. The poet who calls his mind Puzzle is made uneasy by limestone, which doubts his fictions. And Clio the merciful and forgiving does not look as if she ever read the poets.

The Tempest is full of dissolving borders, the actors that melt into thin air, the morning that "steals upon the night, / Melting the darkness," the approaching tide that fills the muddy shore, the *plaudite* in which Prospero asks for the audience's indulgence. Auden's poems are full of absolute borders. His audience exists across an "essential emphatic gulf," and like Alonso to Ferdinand, he writes for you to read when he is gone. Each poem is as cut off from love as John Nower is from the Man-Woman who "appears as a prisoner of war behind barbed wire, in the snow." Whatever would redeem the poem from insignificance lies beyond words, and so in its ritual act of concession each poem announces itself as a border as certain as that between Death and Life.

APPENDIX

The Manuscript Drafts of *New Year Letter*, Part III, Opening Passage

NEW YEAR LETTER

Transcript of manuscript draft of the beginning of part 3, from a holograph notebook (1940–1942) in the possession of the Berg Collection of the New York Public Library (Item J9 in B. C. Bloomfield and Edward Mendelson, eds., *W. H. Auden: A Bibliography: 1924–1969* [Charlottesville, 1972]).

Across the River in the night

Manhattan is ablaze with light

War's ~~Death's~~ shadows dare not criticize

The popular festivities

Alone now I recall, dear friend

The evenings of last weekend

~~When in your house we felt descend~~

~~Upon our little company~~

~~The Dove of Christmas~~

~~The Christmas joy, the blessed Dove~~

When on the little company

That gathered in your house

When in your house we felt descend

~~The~~ Upon us all the Christmas Dove

Of faith and happiness and love

~~As Mozart played and~~

As Schubert sang and Mozart played

And Gluck and food and friendship made
A momentary
~~Our a p---t~~ community

~~A~~ The ~~true~~ Real Republic which must be
all
What ——— the politicians claim

— Even the worst — to be their aim.

New Year Letter

Partial transcript of manuscript draft of the beginning of part 3, from a holograph notebook (1940) in the possession of the Humanities Research Center, University of Texas, Austin, Texas (some marginal notes have been omitted); Item J10 in Bloomfield and Mendelson, *Bibliography.*

But
~~Warm~~ in your house, Elizabeth,

A week ago at the same hour
I
~~We~~ felt the unexpected power.

[page break]

Across East River in the night

Manhattan is ablaze with light
No
~~Lest~~ shadows dares to criticise

The popular festivities,

Hard liquor causes everywhere

A general detente, and Care

For this state function of good-will

Is diplomatically ill.

~~The old year dies a noisy death.~~

~~Alone now, I recall, dear friend,~~

These evenings of last week-end

the dove

When, in your house, we felt descend

~~Upon us all the Christmas dove~~

~~Of faith and happiness and love~~

our

That drove ~~each~~ ragged egos in

~~our~~ the

From ~~his~~ dead-ends of fear and sin

To sit down at the wedding feast,

Put shining garments on the least

Arranged us so that each and all,

The erotic and the logical,

Each felt the placement to be such

That he was honoured overmuch.

And Schubert sang and Mozart played

And Gluck and food and friendship made

Our fortunate community

That real republic which must be

The State

~~What~~ all the politicians claim,

Even the worst, to be their aim.

But last weekend

~~A week ago,~~ Elizabeth

~~Upon~~ Warm in your house, at the same hour

~~Up together at your house,~~

~~We I~~ felt the unexpected power

Index

Alice in Wonderland, 120
Arendt, Hannah, 15
Apostles' Creed, The, 136–37
Auden, W. H.: acts role of Caliban, 31; on art and Christianity, 10–11, 24, 144, 149; his attitude toward literary criticism, ix, xiii; his attitude toward Nazis, 9; death of, 144; emigration of, ix, x, xi, 19–20, 25; letter to his father about *For the Time Being*, 95; mother of, 5n, 10; on "Nature" and "History," 135, 152, 152–53n; his 1930s plays, 11–12, 48; his 1930s poetry, scholarly opinion of, ix–x, 19–20, 20n; on "parable-art," 24–25, 30, 33, 38; *plaudite*, his use of, 73–76, 161, 162; poems of, as *retractio*, x, 165–67; his poetry after 1939, ix–x, 12, 120–26, 160; his relationship with Chester Kallman, 10, 44, 71, 116 (*see also* Kallman, Chester); his relationship with Elizabeth Mayer, 5, 8, 16, 39, 75, 80, 81, 82, 86 (*see also* Mayer, Elizabeth); Renaissance, his ideas about, 62; his return to Anglican Church, x, 8–9; self-deprecation and deference of, 12, 119–26; social and political ideas of, ix, xi, xii, 9; and speech/writing dichotomy, 4, 6, 20–30, 31–33, 39–45; and *veneratio poetarum* (veneration of the poets), 78, 124, 153; visits Spain, 9; wins Pulitzer Prize, Bollingen Prize, and National Book Award, 137
Auden, W. H.: Works
—Manuscripts
drafts of *The Dog beneath the Skin*, 60–61, 70, 82–83, 87; drafts of *For the Time Being*, 90, 91; Manuscript Notebook 1941–42, 85; drafts of *New Year Letter*, 17, 83–85, 169–72; drafts of *The Sea and the Mirror*, 101, 162–63; "Vocation and Society," 71, 95
—Plays and Libretti
The Dance of Death, 47, 56–58, 61, 143; *Delia, or A Masque of Night*, 15, 163–64; *The Dog beneath the Skin*, 30, 31, 47, 50, 58–61, 64, 102; *The Enemies of a Bishop*, 75n; *On the Frontier*, 47, 48, 61–62; *Paid on Both Sides*, 9, 46–47, 55–56, 57, 58, 61, 62, 102, 145, 168; *Paul Bunyan*, 14
—Poems
"A. E. Housman," 68; *Another Time*, 20, 47, 63, 66–70; "As I walked out one evening," 68, 129; "At the Grave of Henry James," 78–79, 153, 166–67; "Autumn 1940," 20; "The Ballad of Barnaby," 3–8, 12, 155, 156, 165; "Cattivo Tempo," 123, 154; "The Cave of Making," xii, xiii, 6, 7–8, 12–13, 79, 153–56, 167; "City without Walls," 14, 15, 16, 106, 109, 110, 130, 157; "Compline," 66, 151, 152, 153, 156; "Dichtung und Wahrheit," 42–44; "Doggerel by a Senior Citizen," 157; "Dover," 68; "Edward Lear," 68; "Epistle to a

Auden, W. H.: Works (*cont.*)
Godson," 5, 119–20; "Epitaph on a Tyrant," 69; "Epithalamion (For Giuseppe Antonio Borgese and Elizabeth Mann, Nov. 23, 1939)," 47, 62–67, 83; "Epithalamion for the wedding of Alan Sinkinson and Iris Snodgrass" (1931), 48–53, 55, 58, 60, 63, 65, 66, 67; *For the Time Being*, 6, 14, 52, 73, 75, 86–98, 111, 159, 161; "Good-bye to the Mezzogiorno," 124–25; "Homage to Clio," 8, 12, 45, 122, 126–27n, 128, 152, 153, 157, 167; *Homage to Clio*, 134; *Horae Canonicae*, 5, 66, 148–53, 156, 157 (*see also* titles of individual poems); "The Horatians," 125–26; "Hunting Season," 121; "In Memory of Sigmund Freud," 46–47, 69–70; "In Memory of W. B. Yeats," 27–29, 69, 159; "In Praise of Limestone," 4–5, 126n, 134–37, 138, 152, 153, 157, 159; "In Sickness and in Health," 70–71; "It was Easter as I walked . . . ," 53–54; "James Honeyman," 69; "Just as his dream foretold . . . ," 54–55; "Lauds," 152–53; *Letter to Lord Byron*, 76–77; "Lullaby," 156–57; "Memorial for the City," 138–48, 152, 157, 159; *New Year Letter*, 5, 8, 14, 16, 17, 20, 29, 30, 73, 75, 76–86, 87, 88, 90, 101, 107, 134, 153, 156, 159, 167; "Ode to Gaea," 123; "Ode to Terminus," 123; "O what is that sound that so thrills the ear," 129; "Oxford," 68, 70; "Precious Five," 122, 126n; "Prime," 149; "Schoolchildren," 68
The Sea and the Mirror: Alonso in, 164–65; anticipation of, 65; Ariel's song in, 115–17; Caliban in, 6, 12, 29, 30–38, 41, 44, 110–15, 136, 146, 161–62, 167; epigraph to, 117, 139, 160, 169; and later poems, 12, 120, 156; and "Memorial for the City," 146; and other long poems, 73–76, 99–100, 101, 159, 167; paratheatrical characters in, 75, 99–101, 159, 161; Prospero in, 102–5; relation of, to *Tempest*, 16–18, 167; silence in, x, 45, 76; structure of, 101–2; and "The Supporting Cast, Sotto Voce," 104–10
"Sext," 150–51; "The Shield of Achilles," 68, 127–33, 148, 162; "Spain 1937," 69; "Spring in Wartime," 20; "A Summer Night," 9, 83–84; "Terce," 149; "A Thanksgiving," 78, 124; " 'The Truest Poetry Is the Most Feigning,' " 8, 39–41, 42, 45; "Till I Will Be Overthrown," 67–68; "Vespers," 151, 158; "Victor," 69; "We, too, had known golden hours," 123; "Who will endure," 159
—Prose
The Dyer's Hand, x, 26, 104n, 126n, 144; *The Enchafèd Flood*, 117, 160; Introduction to *The Poet's Tongue*, 22–23, 24; "Jehovah Housman and Satan Housman," 61; "Psychology and Art To-day," 18, 23–25, 26, 28, 30–31; "The Public v. the Late Mr. William Butler Yeats," 27–29, 159; "Reading," ix; "Romantic or Free?" 30n; *Secondary Worlds*, 10, 30n, 119; *Victorian and Edwardian Poets* (ed.), 117; "The Virgin and the Dynamo," 18–19; "Writing," 21–22, 39
Austen, Jane, 14, 23

Bible, 33, 54, 84. *See also* Luke, Book of; Matthew, Book of
Blair, John, 127n
Blake, William, 15, 79–80, 144
Book of Common Prayer, The, 11, 46, 48, 59, 70, 85, 92
Brontë, Emily, 117, 139, 143, 160, 161
Brown, Terence, 20n

Callan, Edward, 32n, 76n
Carpenter, Humphrey, 17n, 31n
Chaucer, Geoffrey, 166
cummings, e. e., 45

Daalder, Joost, 128n
Dante, 39, 79–80, 81, 82, 143
de Man, Paul, 36n
Donne, John, 22, 42, 156, 166
Dryden, John, 60

Eddins, Dwight, 104n
Eliot, T. S., 8, 9, 10, 23, 40, 44, 88, 110, 144

Fuller, John, 32n, 76n, 127n, 139n, 140n

Goethe, Johann Wolfgang von, 124–25
Gorey, Edward, 3
Greene, Thomas M., 49n
Greville, Fulke, 166

Hacker, Marilyn, 77n
Heaney, Seamus, xi, 20n
Herbert, George, 42, 45
Herrick, Robert, 165–66
Hoffman, Daniel, 3n
Hollander, John, 45
Homer, 127–28, 132, 139
Hopper, Stanley, 126–27n
Horace, 124–26
Hough, Graham, 20n
Housman, A. E., 61
Housman, Lawrence, 61
Hunt, John, 78n, 126n
Hynes, Samuel, 29n, 126–27n

Iolanthe, 14
Isherwood, Christopher, ix, 11

James, Henry, 32
Johnson, Richard, 32n, 76n, 127n
Juliana of Norwich, 138, 139, 140, 147

Kallman, Chester, 163. *See also* Auden, W. H.: relationship with
Keats, John, 52, 128

Larkin, Philip, 20n
Lewars, Kenneth, 35n
Lewis, C. S., 124, 139n
Lienhardt, R. G., 20n
Liturgy of the Hours, 148–49n
Luke, Book of, 33, 54, 83, 84, 89

Matthew, Book of, 33, 54, 83, 84, 89, 93, 97
Mayer, Elizabeth, 5, 8, 17, 77. *See also* Auden, W. H.: relationship with
Menander, 73–74
Mendelson, Edward, 20n, 48n, 54n
Milton, John, 138
Mozart, Wolfgang Amadeus, 14, 71

Ong, Walter Jackson, 21n, 32

Peele, George, 163
Plato, 89
Pope, Alexander, 76–77
praeteritio, 12, 122, 128, 130, 131, 148
Pritchard, William, 20n
Pym, Barbara, 52, 59n

Rimbaud, Arthur, 45
Robson, Jeremy, 20n

Shakespeare, William, 12, 15, 41, 42, 67, 72, 74, 109; *As You Like It*, 11, 39, 42, 109, 161, 162; *Cymbeline*, 14, 16, 103; *Hamlet*, 18; *King Lear*, 18; *Love's Labor's Lost*, 74; *Macbeth*, 141; *Measure for Measure*, 15; *A Midsummer Night's Dream*, 161; *The Tempest*, 15, 16, 18, 31, 60, 65, 73, 75, 100, 101, 102, 105, 162, 167, 168; *Twelfth Night*, 73, 109, 161, 162; *The Winter's Tale*, 11, 42, 58, 164–65
Shelley, Percy Bysshe, 160, 161
Sinkinson, Alan, 49, 58
Sinkinson, Iris, 50
Smith, Stan, 80n
Snodgrass, Arnold, 50
Socrates, 38
Spears, Monroe, 32n, 127n, 162n
Spenser, Edmund, 49
Summers, Claude J., 132–33n

Terence, 74

Williams, Charles, 83, 124, 138n, 140n, 141n
Wordsworth, William, 144

Yeats, W. B., 44, 124, 144, 160